Praise for

What Women Should Know about Letting It Go

"This is no icy Disney princess story! It is a real, relevant, and refreshing read that will encourage your heart, mind, and soul. If you've ever felt overwhelmed with the pressures of yesterday, today, and tomorrow, this book is for you. If worry has ever ravaged your heart, rearranged your vision, or clobbered your God-confidence, this book is for you. If you simply need a fresh reminder that God is able to meet you in the sticky messes of everyday life, this book is for you. Don't miss the message of *Letting It Go*. It will change your life and the lives of those you love."

> —**Gwen Smith,** speaker, worship leader, co-founder of Girlfriends in God, and author of *Broken into Beautiful*

"This is a book for every woman, because we've all been burdened by past hurts, regrets, guilt, and disappointment. Christin Ditchfield invites us to let go of what is holding us back, so we can hold onto the One who holds us together. Christin's teachings are practical, life-giving, and soul-reviving. She's a mentor who points us to true north. Every word of *Letting It Go* is a step in a staircase, bringing us closer to the fullest life in Christ."

> —**Jennifer Dukes Lee,** author of *Love Idol*

"*What Women Should Know about Letting It Go* is a book that makes me want to shout 'Amen!' Christin has nailed it again, masterfully encouraging each of us to let go of the things that impede our walk with Christ and to hold on to what is truly important—grace, peace, and joy. *What Women Should Know* is an indispensable guide that will help you in the challenge!"

> —**Kendra Smiley,** conference speaker and author of *Live Free* and *Heart Clutter*

WHAT WOMEN SHOULD KNOW ABOUT

LETTING IT GO

CHRISTIN DITCHFIELD

WHAT WOMEN SHOULD KNOW ABOUT
LETTING IT GO

BREAKING FREE FROM

THE POWER OF GUILT,

DISCOURAGEMENT,

AND DEFEAT

LEAFWOOD
PUBLISHERS

WHAT WOMEN SHOULD KNOW ABOUT LETTING IT GO

Breaking free from the power of guilt, discouragement, and defeat

LEAFWOOD
P U B L I S H E R S
an imprint of Abilene Christian University Press

Copyright © 2015 by Christin Ditchfield

ISBN 978-0-89112-339-2 | LCCN 2014045229

Printed in the United States of America

Published in association with William K. Jensen Literary Agency, 119 Bampton Court, Eugene, Oregon 97404.

LIBRARY OF CONGRESS CATALOGING-IN-PUBLICATION DATA
Ditchfield, Christin.
  What women should know about letting it go : breaking free from the power of guilt, discourage-
ment, and defeat / Christin Ditchfield.
     pages cm
  Includes bibliographical references and index.
  ISBN 978-0-89112-339-2 (alk. paper)
  1. Christian women--Religious life. 2. Guilt--Religious aspects--Christianity. 3. Consolation. 4. Failure-
-Religious aspects--Christianity. 5. Success--Religious aspects--Christianity. I. Title.
  BV4527.D5765 2015
  248.8'43--dc23
                                                                          2014045229

Cover design by Thinkpen Design, LLC | Interior text design by Sandy Armstrong, Strong Design

Leafwood Publishers is an imprint of Abilene Christian University Press
ACU Box 29138, Abilene, Texas 79699
1-877-816-4455 | www.leafwoodpublishers.com

15 16 17 18 19 20 / 7 6 5 4 3 2 1

Contents

For my sisters,

Regina, Stephanie, and Taylor—

your faithful love and cheerful encouragement

and unwavering support have meant more to me

than you will ever know.

Acknowledgments

A special thank you to my literary agent, Bill Jensen, not only for believing in me and the ministry God's called me to, but for the many hours spent brainstorming the right title and direction of this book.

Thank you to Gary Myers, Mary Hardegree, Laura Homer, Duane Anderson, Seth Shaver, Phil Dosa, and Lettie Morrow—the entire team at Leafwood Publishers—for seeing the need for this book, sharing the vision, and turning it into a reality!

In writing a book for and about women, I can't help but be particularly mindful of the many women God has used to powerfully impact my heart and life. There are those who came into my life for a moment—a brief, but very significant moment—"for such a time as this." There are some who were sent for a season. And there are some who are now and always

will be my "forever" friends. There are those I've known personally and intimately and those I've never met—some who may
even have lived and died before I was ever born, and yet whose
testimonies and wise words have challenged me, encouraged
me, and inspired me.

Then there are the countless women I've met at women's
conferences and retreats around the country, the women who've
read my books or blog or listened to my radio show—and freely
opened their hearts to me. We've learned so much from each
other, as we've walked along the Way. Truly we have become
sisters and friends.

I wish I could list all of these precious women here (and part
of me desperately wants to try), but I know in my heart that it
just isn't possible. There are too many! And I'm sure I would
accidentally leave some out. I can only thank God whenever I
think of these amazing women, pray that He will bless them
abundantly beyond all they can ask or imagine, and try to be
a living tribute—a true reflection of all they have taught me,
and the One they pointed me to.

While I was working on this book, I faced some enormous
challenges—physically, emotionally, and spiritually. (That's
been true of the last ten years, really . . . as I've had surgery
after surgery, followed by months and months of bed rest and
ongoing battles with chronic pain.) Just as I started writing this
time, I fractured my leg—and as soon as it healed, I fractured it
again. There are so many things I've had to let go of lately—and
things I've struggled to hold on to. I want especially to express
my gratitude to those dear friends and family members who

have lifted me up and carried me to Jesus, day after day (Mark 2:1–4). David—especially you!

You all are such an important part of every book I write, every word I speak. I could not do what I do—I would not be who I am—without you.

Most of all, thank You, Jesus. You are a tender Healer, a Faithful Friend, and a Strong and Mighty Savior. Your love has triumphed gloriously!

Introduction

*It takes a lot of courage to show
your dreams to someone else.*

—Erma Bombeck

eep breath.

Are you ready? Here goes: I have a dream.

Not nearly as lofty and noble as Dr. Martin Luther King Jr.'s, but still pretty epic—in its own way.

In this dream (get ready to cue the sunshine and singing birds and forest creatures, because it's more of a fairy tale, really), I get up early in the morning—well before dawn—to spend time sitting at Jesus' feet. I read my Bible, record profound spiritual insights in my journal, and pray powerful intercessory prayers on behalf of my friends and family and the world itself.

After this deeply moving devotional time that fills my heart and spills over into my attitude for the rest of the day, I eagerly move on to tackle the day's to-do list with joyful enthusiasm. Because in days past I have wisely budgeted my time, energy, and resources, my list today is not unreasonable or overwhelming. It's all rewarding, fulfilling, meaningful activity, each item moving me forward, helping me to accomplish all that God's called me to do in my career and ministry. I have time scheduled in there for eating right and exercising, as well as taking care of the ordinary, everyday tasks that keep me organized and on track.

I've also set aside time to connect meaningfully with my friends and family, because these relationships are important to me and I know they need nurturing. I know that if a crisis arises, I can drop everything and be there for the ones I love, without a moment's hesitation. I've done such a good job staying on top of everything in my own life that I can afford to be flexible with my schedule. I'm not irritated or upset by interruptions, because I've built in time for little emergencies and mishaps, as well as divine appointments. It makes me feel good to know I can be Jesus' hands and feet and bless others as He has blessed me.

I even have a little time left over for those energizing, refreshing "me breaks" that women's magazines are always going on about. I take a walk on the beach or read a few chapters of a good book or savor a steaming hot cup of coffee or tea. In the evening, I give an hour or two to one of my pet projects—a craft I've seen on Pinterest and wanted to try, or that novel I've always wanted to write.

(This is a *dream*, remember!)

At the end of the day, as I drop into bed, I count my blessings with a thankful heart. I feel such satisfaction, such contentment. This day I have lived intentionally, purposefully, passionately. Fully. And so I know I can fall asleep easily and sleep peacefully.

I do not lie awake at night, tossing and turning, feeling guilty about all the things I didn't get done . . . about having wasted my time or wasted my life. I'm not dreading tomorrow—either the number on the scale or the number of things on my to-do list—because I know I've made good choices and had a great day. And tomorrow will be even better!

I don't clench my jaw or grind my teeth or hold my breath worrying about my life, my friends' and family's lives, the world as it turns. Because I trust Jesus implicitly. I know He's got it all safely in His hands.

Looking back over the day, I don't really have any regrets— because I didn't do anything wrong. I mean, nobody's perfect, of course—but I didn't lose my temper, I wasn't argumentative or envious or lazy or selfish or unkind. I took any stray thoughts captive and kept my eyes on Jesus throughout the day.

Speaking of stray thoughts, in my dream, I do not suddenly remember some terrible mistake from my past, some humiliating failure, some sinful behavior. I don't lie there in my bed, reliving the horror of it all, cringing with embarrassment, burning with guilt and shame. Nor do I start reliving the wrong that's been done to me—those cruel words, that hateful act, the betrayal, the rejection, the abandonment or abuse. I don't lie there churning as I relive the injustice of it all, making my case, arguing my cause, defending myself. I'm not imagining all the things that I wish I would have or could have or should have done, should have said.

I don't vacillate between feeling unfairly ignored or overlooked by God, rejected or abandoned by Him—envious of all the blessings He's given others—and feeling that I'm such a disappointment to Him. Such a miserable, wretched sinner. That I'm so awful. So ugly and unlovely and unlovable.

In my dream, I don't compare myself to other women, one way or another. I don't feel deeply inferior *or* smugly superior.

(One minute the prodigal, the next minute the elder brother.) I believe that I'm a sinner saved by grace, a woman who loves much because she's been forgiven much.

And that's enough for me.

See what I mean? It really is an epic dream.

I keep trying to make it come true. I keep trying to have this elusive perfect day. Trying and trying and trying. But it never happens.

Half the time I oversleep just a little, and it's ruined before it's even begun.

As silly as it sounds when I put it on paper, I know that this dream—or at least some variation of it—isn't just my dream. It's one that many women share. My sisters, my friends. We all dream of having our own version of a beautifully perfect day (reasonably perfect, we tell ourselves), a perfect life. A perfect world.

For myself, I know I often feel caught—torn between the sinful, imperfect woman I am and the woman I so desperately long to be. The woman I sometimes am, or pretend to be. The woman whom Jesus sees, the woman I will one day be.

And often I feel stuck. Unable to move forward, unable to make any real progress in my journey with Jesus. Falling and failing over and over again. (All I have to do is pull out my old journals and look at my New Year's resolutions for the last twenty years. I could have saved myself some trouble if—instead of writing it all down again—I just copied the list every year and changed the date.)

Back to my dream: I need to let it go.

If I want to be free to be the woman God created me to be, I need to let a lot of things go. Things like impossible standards and unrealistic expectations. Guilt, shame, and regret.

Or else I'll stay stuck forever. In this life, anyway.

That's not how I want to live . . . caught. Trapped. Stuck.

I want to let it go.

But how?

How do I let it go?

What does "letting it go" look like in real life? In my life?

And is "letting it go" the end of it—or is there something more to it?

Aren't there some things I'm supposed to be holding on to? I seem to recall that there are lots of Scriptures with words to that effect. Challenging me, encouraging me, urging me not to settle for less than the freedom, the victory, the richly full and overflowing life Jesus has promised me.

These are things I've been thinking about and praying about a lot lately.

I wouldn't say I have all the answers. Honestly, I haven't arrived. But I've finally been making some progress. I've been learning things—sometimes as much from my failures as my successes, by trial and error. I've been learning from the lives of great men and women of the faith, from wise friends and godly mentors. Learning from Scripture and from Jesus Himself, growing in my love relationship with Him.

That's what I hope to share with you in this book. I would love to encourage your heart—as mine has been encouraged. And maybe save you a few steps on your journey. Help you get unstuck a little faster than I have. Because the truth is, we don't have to stay stuck in an endless cycle of failure, discouragement, and defeat. We all have a choice. We can choose to let the past (yesterday or years ago) define us and confine us. Or we can let it refine us. We can also choose to let it go and leave it behind us.

We let it go so that we can hold on to something much better. *Someone* much better.

Someone who will never let go of us.

"In my distress I called to the LORD; I cried to my God for help. . . . He reached down from on high and took hold of me" (Ps. 18:6a, 16a).

Chapter One

Letting Go of Guilt, Shame, and Regret

The only difference between the saint and the sinner is that every saint has a past, and every sinner has a future.

—Oscar Wilde

There's a scene in one movie adaptation of *Pride and Prejudice* in which Mr. Bennet reflects on his failings as a father. Because of his permissive parenting, his fifteen-year-old daughter Lydia is now openly "living in sin" with a gambling, drinking, blackmailing scoundrel. The situation is dire, threatening to destroy not only Lydia, but her entire family—especially her four sisters, whose chances for love and marriage will be ruined by Lydia's soiled reputation. ("Who would want to connect themselves with *such* a family?") Elizabeth is worried that her father will be overcome by his guilt and grief. He reassures her: "I am heartily ashamed of myself, Lizzie. But don't despair; it'll pass, and no doubt more quickly than it should."[1]

That wry observation has always resonated with me, because I know in my own life there are times when I've felt tremendous guilt—great remorse over some particular sin, some attitude or action or behavior that I've deeply regretted. For a few hours or a few days, that is. In the moment, I've resolved never to give in to that sin, never to make that terrible mistake again. Then

I fall right back into the very same sin, when the memory of those guilty feelings has faded.

But much more often, I've experienced the kind of guilt and shame and regret that sticks with me. Shadows me. Haunts me. Hinders me. I'm so preoccupied with it, so paralyzed by it. I just can't get past it, can't get free of it. Can't seem to let it go. It reminds me of the title of a popular rock song: "Stuck in a Moment That You Can't Get Out Of."[2]

I've been there. Lord knows, I've been there. I know you have, too.

For some reason, we keep replaying the fateful scene over and over—that humiliating mistake, that terrible decision, those awful words, that grievous sin. Wincing, cringing, sometimes even weeping over the things we said or did long before we knew better—before we knew Jesus—as well as things we've said or done since, when we absolutely did know.

If only we could just click "undo" or "delete" in real life.

But we can't.

So, instead, we verbally flog ourselves.

I can't believe it . . .

Why did I do that? Say that?

Why didn't I do this? Say that?

What on earth was I thinking?

What's wrong with me?

I'll never be able to forgive myself. How could I be so stupid? So foolish? So blind? So selfish? So wrong?

As if there were any good answers to these questions. As if asking them could bring us the relief we're looking for, longing for. It still wouldn't change the past—whether the past is twenty years ago or twenty minutes ago, whether it was one awful, life-changing, devastating decision or a series of everyday failures that pile up to form a mountain of guilt, shame, and regret.

As long as we continue to carry the weight of it on our own shoulders, we will stagger and stumble through life— rather than running free. Dancing with grace and courage and strength. Becoming the women we were created to be.

Faith is a living, daring confidence in God's grace, so sure and certain that a man could stake his life on it a thousand times.
—Martin Luther

Countless books have been written—hymns sung, sermons preached—on the subject of grace. The theology of grace. The staggering truth that God so passionately, devotedly, magnificently loved the world—you and me and everyone in it—that He sent His only Son to die a cruel and agonizing death on the cross to pay for our sin. He took the punishment in our place, so that He could forgive us and reconcile us to Himself. Not because we earned it. Not because we proved ourselves worthy or deserving in any way. There's nothing we could ever do to be good enough or worthy enough or deserving enough. Not then. Not now. Not ever.

That's what makes it so incredible, so amazing, so mind-boggling, so incomprehensible.

"Come now, let us reason together, says the LORD: though your sins are like scarlet, they shall be as white as snow" (Isa.

1:18a ESV). Later in the book, He goes on to say, "I, even I, am he who blots out your transgressions, for my own sake, and remembers your sins no more" (Isa. 43:25). And in the New Testament, we learn: "When God our Savior revealed his kindness and love, he saved us, not because of the righteous things we had done, but because of his mercy. He washed away our sins, giving us a new birth and new life through the Holy Spirit" (Titus 3:4–5 NLT).

Horatio Spafford captured this truth so beautifully in the third verse of his beautiful hymn, "It Is Well with My Soul":

> My sin—oh, the bliss of this glorious thought—
> My sin, not in part but the whole,
> Is nailed to the cross, and I bear it no more,
> Praise the Lord, praise the Lord, O my soul![3]

This is the gospel—the very foundation of our faith. If we know this, if we believe this, why is it so hard to let go of our guilt, shame, and regret? Jesus says He has forgiven us, so why can't we forgive ourselves?

You know, guilt is actually supposed to be a gift. Good guilt, that is. True guilt. Healthy guilt. It lets us know when we've done wrong. It points us to the truth. It keeps us humble, instead of haughty and proud, like the self-righteous Pharisees. It reminds us constantly that we are sinners in need of a Savior—and that we have one. We have a strong and mighty Savior whose grace is greater than our sin. It keeps us overflowing with love and gratitude to Him (or at least it can—it should). And if we let it, guilt will teach us—it will help us learn from our mistakes. It serves as a deterrent. If we can't be "good for goodness sake," then we can at least be good to avoid the pain—the discomfort of a guilty conscience, along with the other consequences.

As Brennan Manning writes, "Healthy guilt is one which acknowledges the wrong done and feels remorse, but then is free to embrace the forgiveness that has been offered. Healthy guilt focuses on the realization that all has been forgiven, the wrong has been redeemed."[4] And 2 Corinthians 7:10 explains, "For godly grief *and* the pain God is permitted to direct, produce a repentance that leads *and* contributes to salvation *and* deliverance from evil, and it never brings regret; but worldly grief (the hopeless sorrow that is characteristic of the pagan world) is deadly [breeding and ending in death]" (AMP).

Worldly grief. Hopeless sorrow. Unhealthy guilt—or healthy guilt that we respond to in unhealthy ways. That's when we hold on to our guilt instead of confessing our sin, repenting of it, and letting it go—leaving it with Jesus.

That's what trips us up. That's what knocks us down. Manning says:

> When we wallow in guilt, remorse, and shame over
> real or imagined sins of the past, we are disdaining
> God's gift of grace. Preoccupation with self is
> always a major component of unhealthy guilt and
> recrimination. It stirs our emotions, churning in
> self-destructive ways, closes us in upon the mighty
> citadel of self, leads to depression and despair,
> and preempts the presence of a compassionate
> God. The language of unhealthy guilt is harsh. It is
> demanding, abusing, criticizing, rejecting, accusing,

blaming, condemning, reproaching, and scolding. It
is one of impatience and chastisement. Christians
are shocked and horrified because they have failed.
Unhealthy guilt becomes bigger than life.[5]

But God isn't at all shocked or horrified or even disappointed
when we fail. "This is how we know that we belong to the truth
and how we set our hearts at rest in his presence: If our hearts
condemn us, we know that God is greater than our hearts, and
he knows everything" (1 John 3:19–20 NIV 2011).

Everything.

He knows it all. He sees it all. Nothing in all creation is
hidden from His sight (Heb 4:13).

Psalm 103:13–14 tells us, "As a father has compassion on
his children, so the LORD has compassion on those who fear
him; for he knows how we are formed, he remembers that we
are dust." He understands our weakness, our frailty. He knows
our hearts. He sees us for who we really are—who He created us
to be. And He loves us utterly and completely unconditionally.

It's one thing to feel convicted—to know that you've been
wrong or done wrong and that you need to make things right.
It's another thing to feel condemned. Hopelessly awaiting the
inevitable punishment for your sins.

*"There is now no condemnation for those who are in Christ
Jesus"* (Rom. 8:1).

Philip Yancey points out: "The way to get rid of [guilt] is
not to get rid of the guilt feelings. It is to get rid of the wrong
that you did that caused the guilt feelings."[6]

And how do we do that?

Bring it to Jesus. Big things and small things. Obvious, everybody-knows, anyone-can-see-it things and deepest, darkest secret things. "If we confess our sins, he is faithful and just and will forgive us our sins and purify us from all unrighteousness" (1 John 1:9).

You can't read the Gospels without seeing His love and mercy and grace. His compassion for those caught in sin, bowed down with guilt and shame. He was called "a friend of sinners" because He deliberately sought out those who were lost . . . society's outcasts, the undesirables, the untouchables. The ragamuffins. He went looking for them and He found them. No matter who they were or what they had done, if they were desperate for hope, hungry for truth, longing for help—He welcomed them. He received them with open arms, just as they were. He loved them. He forgave them. He restored them.

This same Jesus invites us to come to Him, too.

Even after we have come, even after we've said yes to Him, even after we've been cleansed and forgiven and made new . . . He knows we're still going to fall into temptation sometimes. We're going to mess up, big-time. We'll make a lot of mistakes.

Still, He says, "Come!"

Because of Jesus, we don't have to live lives filled with guilt and shame and regret. Our mistakes don't define us. We are so much more than that bad choice, that poor response, that selfish or angry or rebellious moment, more than any or all of our failures and mistakes. Past, present, or future.

*My heroes are the ones who survived doing it wrong, who
made mistakes, but recovered from them.*

—Bono

In John 11, we find two familiar figures who are most often
remembered for their mistakes...down through the centuries,
their names have become synonymous with their momentary
failures. And yet in this one chapter, we see that they were so
much more. Jesus knew them for who they really were. It's
time we did, too.

First there's Thomas. "Doubting Thomas." He's the skeptic
who once said, "Unless I see the nail marks in his hands and
put my finger where the nails were, and put my hand into his
side, I will not believe" (John 20:25). Through the centuries,
many have condemned him for his lack of faith, while others
have sympathized and rationalized why he was—"understand-
ably"—slow to believe.

But that was just one faithless moment.

In John 11:1–16, the other disciples try to discourage Jesus
from returning to Judea. They're afraid and unwilling to go, even
to help a friend like Lazarus, because the Pharisees might try
to stone Jesus again. But Thomas puts an end to the discussion
by boldly declaring that he's willing to follow Jesus anywhere,
even to His death: "Let us also go, that we may die with him."

And he meant it. Because that's just what he did—he went,
and he took the other disciples with him.

Thomas had real courage. Real faith. Real commitment to the cause of Christ. He led by example. And he followed up his words with his actions. History tells us he went on to take the gospel throughout the Roman Empire and became the first missionary to India. Even in that instance when his faith failed him—however briefly—we see that he was afterward quick to humble himself, quick to repent and believe. Thomas was not defined by his mistakes. Because of Jesus, he was so much more.

Then there's Martha. Every Christian woman knows the story of Martha—the woman who was so busy doing *for* Jesus that she neglected to spend time *with* Him. The busy woman bustling around the kitchen, caught up in the cares of this life, nagging and whining and complaining—instead of taking the time (like her sister Mary) to sit at Jesus' feet.

Sometimes, the way we tell the story, you'd think Mary was Cinderella, and Martha one of the ugly stepsisters. But in John 11:17–43, it's a different scene. Mary is the one whose faith fails her, whose emotions (anger, hurt, frustration, fear, and despair) get the better of her. Mary only comes to Jesus when He calls for her.

But Martha is seeking Him; she's standing out there on the outskirts of town, waiting for Him. And when He asks her if she trusts Him, if she believes in Him, she answers with one of the most powerful, unequivocal declarations of faith in all the Gospels. She may not have known what He was going to do (v. 39), but she knew who He was: "Yes, Lord, I have believed [I do believe] that You are the Christ (the Messiah, the Anointed One), the Son of God, [even He] Who was to come into the world. [It is for Your coming that the world has waited]" (John 11:27 AMP).

In spite of her attitude on that one "terrible, horrible, no good, very bad day," Martha was a woman of faith. A woman of strength and character and dignity and integrity. We see that throughout this story. She was not defined by her past mistakes. Because of Jesus, she was so much more.

Painful as it may be, a significant emotional event can be the catalyst for choosing a direction that serves us—and those around us—more effectively. Look for the learning.

—Louisa May Alcott

Flip through the pages of Scripture, and you'll see so many men and women who were all too human. They had serious character flaws. They made major mistakes. Before *and* after God called them. But God still worked in them and through them to accomplish great and mighty things for His kingdom. In 2 Corinthians 4:7, Paul explains, "We have this treasure [the light of Christ] in jars of clay to show that this all-surpassing power is from God and not from us." Later on, he said, "Therefore I will boast all the more gladly about my weaknesses, so that Christ's power may rest on me. . . . For when I am weak, then I am strong" (2 Cor. 12:9b–10).

In our weakness, God's power and strength are revealed. Through the cracks in our broken, messed-up lives, His light shines brightly. The world can see Jesus in us. We don't have to be perfect or pious or put together to bring Him glory. We just need to be willing and available. The amazing thing is that each and every day, God uses ordinary people like us to do extraordinary things for Him.

What about you?

Will you let your mistakes and failures define you? Or will you choose to believe what Jesus says about you—will you choose to see yourself as He sees you? Flawed and frail and imperfect at times—but deeply beloved. The apple of His eye. His priceless masterpiece, His precious possession. Clothed in His righteousness, spotless and pure before Him. Radiant with His love, His joy, His peace. Fearfully and wonderfully made. Gloriously individual and unique. Day by day becoming a beautiful reflection of Him.[7]

Bible Study

At the end of each chapter, you'll find questions like these to help you reflect on the biblical principles we've discussed and apply them to your own life. You may want to record your responses in a separate notebook or journal.

1. How much would you say you wrestle with feelings of guilt, shame, and regret?

☐ Once in a while
☐ Fairly frequently
☐ Constantly
☐ It's crippling me

2. What kind of guilt or shame do you wrestle with the most? Assign a percentage of time (out of 100) to each of these categories:

_____ Specific events (choices, actions, attitudes, or behaviors) from your past

_____ Daily events (cheating on your diet, losing your temper, running late)

_____ External guilt (pressure from our culture or the media or from others to know more, be more, do more, look more . . .)

_____ Internal guilt (deep-seated feelings of guilt, shame, or regret for failing at things you really have little or no control over, circumstances you didn't orchestrate and can't change)

3. Have you shared these things openly and honestly with Jesus? He already knows—but you'll feel better if you tell it to Him. Take a few moments now to pray over anything and everything you feel guilty about or ashamed of—you can write your prayer in your journal or just speak from your heart.

If you've confessed and repented of these things before and they still trouble you, ask yourself if there's a reason (if you haven't been completely honest about it or if you were sorry you got caught—sorry it made you look bad—more than you were sorry you did wrong). Although you don't need to continually repent for the same sins over and over again, you can always bring them to Jesus, whenever they trouble you. We'll talk about some other strategies in the next chapter.

4. Look up Isaiah 64:8 and Jeremiah 18:1–7. What does God do with "marred" or broken vessels, or as Patsy Clairmont calls them, "cracked pots"?

5. Take a look at Romans 8:28–29 in the New Living Translation:

> And we know that God causes everything to work together for the good of those who love God and are called according to his purpose for them. For God knew his people in advance, and he chose them to become like his Son, so that his Son would be the firstborn among many brothers and sisters.

What does God cause to work together for good? What does that include?

What is the ultimate goal or purpose?

Even the things we feel most guilty or ashamed of—the things we most regret—can be used by God to teach us and mold us and make us more like His precious Son!

6. Choose one of the following verses—or one mentioned previously in the chapter—to memorize and meditate on this week:

Acts 3:19	Romans 8:1
Lamentations 3:22–23	Isaiah 43:18–19
1 John 1:9	Psalm 34:5
Jeremiah 29:11	Philippians 3:12–14

7. Take a few moments to record any further thoughts or reflections in your journal.

Chapter Two

Holding On to Grace

Jesus comes not for the super-spiritual but for the wobbly and the weak-kneed who know they don't have it all together, and who are not too proud to accept the handout of amazing grace.

—Brennan Manning

salm 103:10–12 tells us that God "does not treat us as our sins deserve. . . . For as high as the heavens are above the earth, so great is his love for those who fear him; as far as the east is from the west, so far has he removed our transgressions from us."

Nazi Holocaust survivor, author, and speaker Corrie ten Boom was fond of quoting the verse in Micah 7:19 that says God has "cast all our sins into the depths of the sea" (ESV). Often she would add that He had put up a sign that reads NO FISHING. It's a powerful picture of a truth that can be so hard to grasp.

We know that God says—pretty emphatically—that He has forgiven our sins. But for some reason, we keep fishing them up. So often we find ourselves reliving the horror, the embarrassment, and the humiliation over and over again. It's one thing to know in our heads that we are forgiven. It's another thing to know it—to believe it—in the very depths of our hearts and souls. We may be grateful that we're not going to hell when we die, but many of us are living right now in a hell of our own making—staggering under the burden of our guilt and shame.

So how do we overcome the disconnect between our heads and our hearts? When the sins of the past come flashing back, how do we resist the urge to go fishing? How do we break free?

I can tell you right now what *won't* work. At least what hasn't worked for me. These are some of the more unhealthy and ultimately unhelpful strategies:

- Rationalizing, minimizing, or making excuses for my sin—or blame-shifting.
- Punishing myself, sabotaging myself, or seeing to it that I end up in the misery I feel I deserve.
- Numbing myself, medicating myself (with food, for instance—the way some people use drugs or alcohol), distracting myself, or escaping from myself in endless online shopping, hours of social media, games or puzzles on my iPad, and tons of Netflix or TV.
- Making over-the-top sacrifices, attempting rigid self-discipline, or doing lots of good deeds.

None of these things have the power to set me free. They just add to my misery. "When the kindness and love of God our Savior appeared, he saved us, not because of righteous things we had done, but because of his mercy" (Titus 3:4–5). The word translated "mercy" is *eleos*—meaning an action "taken out of compassion for others or undertaken to alleviate their misery or relieve their suffering."[1] Mercy is a word we often find paired with grace, or *charis*, which means "to rejoice; that which causes joy or delight."[2] It's the gratitude, the thankfulness we feel as we experience God's delight in us. His loving-kindness toward us. His unearned, unmerited favor.

Grace, in turn, is often paired in Scripture with the Greek word *eirene*—peace. A deep sense of well-being.

> *Nothing is too hard for God,*
> *no sin too difficult for His love to overcome,*
> *not a failure but He can make it a success.*
> —Oswald Chambers

How do we experience that peace? How do we break free from the power of guilt and shame, discouragement and defeat?

It's not just about letting it go; it's about what we choose to hold on to.

First and foremost, we need to choose to hold on to grace.

Hebrews 4:14 and 16 explain, "Let us hold firmly to what we believe. . . . So let us come boldly to the throne of our gracious God. There we will receive his mercy, and we will find grace to help us when we need it most" (NLT).

Here's how I think we do that—how we let go of our guilt and shame and hold on to grace.

Recognize the difference between true guilt and false guilt. True guilt is what you feel when you have done wrong. Call it your conscience or the conviction of the Holy Spirit. Your attitude, your actions, or your behavior—these are things that you are responsible for and have control over.

False guilt is what you feel when you take responsibility for things that are not in your power or under your control—things that really aren't your fault. For example, children who feel responsible for their parents' divorce, victims of abuse who are told or who otherwise come to believe that they somehow invited, provoked, or deserved the abuse. Survivors of trage-dies and disasters who feel guilty that they lived when others didn't. Or those of us who have come to believe that we have the power to stop bad things from happening to the people we love—or that we are somehow responsible for their choices, their problems, or their actions, attitudes, and behaviors, as well as their overall health, happiness, and well-being. (We'll talk more about the illusion of control in Chapter Seven.) False guilt is also what we feel when we fail to meet our own impos-sible standards and unrealistic expectations. (More on this in Chapter Three.)

Only God is all-knowing, all-present, all-powerful. Only He is perfectly perfect. And we are not Him.

Bring it into the light. Sin thrives in secrecy; guilt and shame only grow in the darkness. When we are honest with God, with ourselves, and with others, we don't have to be afraid of being uncovered or exposed. We take away the enemy's source of emotional or spiritual "blackmail"—that big, ugly stick he likes to beat us with. We can see more clearly when we hold everything up to the light of His truth. (See 2 Cor. 4:6, Rom. 13:12, 1 Cor. 4:5, Eph. 5:8–11, and 1 Pet. 2:9.)

So tell Jesus the things you're sorry for, the things you feel guilty or ashamed of. He already knows—but it helps you to come clean. It removes those invisible barriers that seem to keep you from experiencing His presence. You can tell Him silently in the quiet of your heart, or out loud in prayer, or in the pages of your journal. Whatever feels most natural to you.

Some things perhaps should stay just between you and Him. But other things you may want to share with a spouse, an accountability partner, a trusted friend, or a circle of friends and family. Those who will listen compassionately, without judging or condemning you. Those who will lovingly point you to the truth, praying with you and for you. When you share openly and honestly about your struggles, you give them permission to be open and honest about their struggles. And you'll find you are not alone!

I realize it's possible you may not have anyone in your life right now who is willing or able to serve as a good sounding board for you. Your friends and family may be too involved to be objective or may not be able to understand or relate to the complexity of the issues you're working through. You may want to consider talking to a Christian counselor or therapist—someone who can remain objective and give you some much-needed—and, ideally, biblical—perspective. (For more information, see the section called When Do I Need an Accountability Partner, a Life Coach, or a Licensed Therapist? And check out the Recommended Resources at the end of the book.)

Remember that grace trumps both karma and consequences. Eastern religions teach that all our pain and suffering is caused by our sin—whether in this life or a past life—and in the end, we all get what we deserve. And new age mystics tell us whatever we put out into the universe is what we will get in return. The Bible teaches us the principle that our actions have consequences—we reap what we sow (Gal. 6:7). But then it teaches us there is a greater law at work: the law of love—God's for us, not ours for Him. And it teaches us the triumph of His grace. "Those who are in Christ Jesus"—we don't get what we deserve (Rom. 8:1).

When we experience pain and suffering in this life, it is not because we are paying for our sins—that debt has already been paid. Sometimes (though not always), God does allow us to experience the natural consequences of our actions. And that can be tough. Sometimes He allows us to undergo necessary discipline (training and correction). But it's never punishment for our sins. Never punitive or vindictive or retaliatory on His part. And even when the trials and tribulations we experience are our fault, He still offers us His mercy in the midst of it. He covers us with His grace. He gives us His peace and strength. No one in Scripture was *ever* rebuked for earnestly seeking God or asking Him for help—regardless of the mess he got himself into or how richly she deserved it. But many, many people were rebuked for stubbornly refusing to seek His face, choosing to stoically suffer the consequences of their sin rather than ask for and receive His mercy and grace.

Learn from your failures and mistakes. Everyone stumbles and falls or fails. Everyone misses the mark. Everyone makes mistakes. You can be discouraged and defeated by your mistakes—or you can make them serve you, make them work for you! Let those painful experiences teach you. Let them help you to grow and mature as a woman, and in your faith.

When I was younger, I could never understand people who claimed they had no regrets. How could you not regret things you said or did—choices you made—that ended up hurting you or hurting others? How could you not regret disobeying or dishonoring the God who loved you and gave Himself for you? I still don't know that that's possible for me. But I think I understand now what they meant. I can honestly say that I'm grateful for my mistakes—as painful as they were (or are)— because of what I've learned from them. Yes, it was hard. It *is* hard. But it sure beats the alternative. I've met some people who've never learned not to do this or say that or behave in a certain way. They haven't learned from their mistakes. And they continue to leave a trail of destruction—and an awful lot of wounded people—in their wake. I'm glad that I know better now, that I know not to make some of those same mistakes, even if that knowledge came at a hefty price.

And I know that in God's economy, nothing is wasted. He uses it all—even my failures and mistakes—in the process of making me into the image of His precious Son. He compares it to a refiner's fire (Isa. 48:10). He turns up the heat Himself—or allows it to be turned up—so that all of my impurities and imperfections, all my faults and flaws rise to the surface. That's where they can be seen clearly and dealt with thoroughly. I know He's at work in me and through me, and "when he has tested me, I will come forth as gold" (Job 23:10).

You build on failure. You use it as a stepping stone. Close the door on the past. You don't try to forget the mistake, but you don't dwell on it. You don't let it have any of your energy, or any of your time, or any of your space.

—Johnny Cash

Resist the enemy of your soul. Revelation 12:10 tells us that one of the devil's names is "the accuser" (the "accuser of our brothers and sisters" [NLT])—and that night and day he brings accusations against us before God. But God will have none of it, and neither should we. We know that the blood of Jesus was shed for us; we've been forgiven and set free. And she whom the Son has set free is free indeed! (See John 8:31–32.)

The psalmist prayed: "May your unfailing love come to me, O LORD, your salvation according to your promise; then I will answer the one who taunts me, for I trust in your word" (Ps. 119:41–42). His salvation has come to us! And the way to respond to the enemy, to our accuser—whether he whispers in our hearts or speaks through those around us—is with the Word of God. Fill your heart and mind with Scripture. Meditate on it. Memorize it. Use it to "take captive every thought" instead of letting your thoughts and feelings take control of you (2 Cor. 10:5).

Fill your heart, your home, your car, your office, your MP3 player with praise and worship. (See the Recommended Resources for some suggestions.) Constantly thank God for His mercy and His grace. And remember what it says in Isaiah 54:17: "'No weapon forged against you will prevail, and you will refute every tongue that accuses you. This is the heritage of the servants of the LORD, and this is their vindication from me,' declares the LORD."

Romans 16:20 tells us, "The God of peace will soon crush Satan under your feet. The grace of our Lord Jesus be with you."

Refuse to wallow. Don't even go down that dark, dark road. Both Judas and Peter betrayed Jesus. Judas was so ashamed, he hanged himself. Peter was so ashamed, he humbled himself and was forgiven, redeemed, and restored. "He gives us more and more grace . . . gives grace [continually] to the lowly (those who are humble enough to receive it)" (James 4:6 AMP).

Don't allow yourself to wallow in self-pity, self-doubt, self-recrimination, self-condemnation—self-anything! Because wallowing is not the same as true humility. It doesn't produce the fruit of repentance, a harvest of righteousness and peace (Heb. 12:11). Take your eyes off yourself completely, and fix them firmly on Jesus. Then look around for others who are struggling—people you can help or encourage or comfort or strengthen or support. It's one of the most powerful, most effective ways to change the channel in your head!

Let it lead you to love Jesus more—much more. All our sin, all our guilt, all our shame—He took it on Himself. He lovingly humbled himself and laid aside His divine glory and majesty to become one of us. He patiently endured the rejection, the scorn, the ridicule, the shame. And then He willingly suffered a cruel and agonizing death on the cross, taking the punishment we deserve, in our place. Listen to Him explain:

> The Spirit of the Sovereign LORD is on me,
>   because the LORD has anointed me
>   to preach good news to the poor.
> He has sent me to bind up the brokenhearted,
>   to proclaim freedom for the captives
>   and release from darkness for the prisoners,
>   to proclaim the year of the LORD's favor
>   and the day of vengeance of our God,

> to comfort all who mourn,
> and provide for those who grieve in Zion—
> to bestow on them a crown of beauty
>   instead of ashes,
> the oil of gladness
>   instead of mourning,
> and a garment of praise
>   instead of a spirit of despair.
>   (Isa. 61:1–3; Luke 4:18–19)

This is why He came. Do you hear the tenderness, the kindness and compassion? The justice mixed with mercy, the amazing grace?

She heard it. And it absolutely captivated her. Captured her heart completely.

She is known now as she was then—as "a sinful woman." A social outcast, a pariah. Yet she dared to make her way to the house of Simon the Pharisee (Luke 7:36–50). Maybe she came on impulse, out of a sudden, overwhelming desire to say thank you. On the way out the door, she grabbed the only thing she had of any value—an alabaster jar of expensive perfume. What else could she give Him in return for what He had given her? Maybe she realized—as she got closer—that she hadn't even thought of what she would do or what she would say when she saw Him. If she saw Him. If she could get through. Then again, maybe she had practiced the words over and over, all the way—what she would tell Jesus, if she got a moment to talk to Him, before she was pulled away.

The moment came, but the words didn't. Just tears.

Lots and lots of tears.

> As she stood behind him at his feet weeping, she
> began to wet his feet with her tears. Then she
> wiped them with her hair, kissed them and poured
> perfume on them. (Luke 7:38 NIV 2011)

Simon wasn't moved by her expression of love and gratitude. Though he said nothing, he judged her in his heart—and judged Jesus for not judging her, too.

Jesus knew. He confronted Simon with a story—a parable about the true nature of gratitude. Then He looked at the woman and said: "I tell you, her sins—and they are many—have been forgiven, so she has shown me much love. But a person who is forgiven little shows only little love" (Luke 7:47 NLT).

To put it another way: she who (in her self-justification and self-righteousness) thinks she has been forgiven little—she loves little. But she who knows the true state of her own soul, who acknowledges her sin, her guilt, her shame, who recognizes her desperate need for a strong and mighty Savior, she who knows she has been forgiven much loves much.

Which woman would you rather be?

See, it's true. All that guilt and shame and regret . . . it doesn't have to hinder you or hobble you or hold you back. It really can be a gift, if it leads you to the feet of Jesus. If you can let it go and leave it there. And learn to live in the light of His love, His mercy, His grace.

I do not at all understand the mystery of grace—
only that it meets us where we are but does not
leave us where it found us.

—Anne Lamott

Bible Study

1. Looking back, what are some of the unhealthy—and ultimately unhelpful—ways you've tried to deal with guilt, shame,
and regret?

2. How effective have these strategies been? What have you
experienced as a result?

3. Which of the healthier strategies discussed in this chapter
could you start putting into practice today? Can you think of
any other strategies that have worked or might work for you?

4. Consider trying a visual exercise like this one. On the bottom two-thirds of a sheet of paper (or small poster board), list all the things you feel guilty about or ashamed of or that you regret—everything you can think of, big or small.

When you've finished, pray over each item briefly—confessing it and repenting of it. Then cover it all with dark blue marker to represent "the depths of the sea" (Micah 7:19). In the space at the top, draw a simple sign that says NO FISHING! Whenever the memory of a particular sin comes rushing back, point to the page or poster and remind yourself to leave it where it is.

5. Look up 2 Corinthians 12:7–10. What kind of battle was the Apostle Paul embroiled in? What did he try to do about it?

Countless Bible scholars have speculated as to what Paul's "thorn" might have been. Some insist it was a physical weakness, while others believe it was spiritual—a specific kind of temptation. Still others suggest it was the memory of the Christians he persecuted and killed before he came to faith in Christ himself. Or the fact that he was constantly regarded with suspicion and distrust, whenever he encountered those who could not forget his past.

Whatever it was, the thorn wasn't going anywhere. So how did Paul learn to deal with it? What attitude did he have?

6. Choose one of the following verses—or one mentioned previously in the chapter—to memorize and meditate on this week.

Psalm 32:5   Psalm 103:12

Psalm 51:10   2 Corinthians 10:3–5

Psalm 130:3–4   Ephesians 1:7

Philippians 4:8   Job 23:10

7. Take a few moments to record any further thoughts or reflections in your journal.

Chapter Three

Letting Go of Impossible Standards and Unrealistic Expectations

I do not think there is anyone who needs God's help and grace as much as I do. Sometimes I feel so helpless and weak. I think that is why God uses me. Because I cannot depend on my own strength, I rely on Him twenty-four hours a day. If the day had even more hours, then I would need His help and grace during those hours as well.

—**Mother Teresa**

An Australian hospice nurse named Bronnie Ware spent several years caring for patients who had less than twelve weeks to live. As they realized they were really and truly dying, many of them had revelations—epiphanies—about life. Things they wish they had discovered much, much earlier. Ware decided to take notes, so that she and we could learn from them. She made a list of the top five regrets of the dying, the themes that emerged over and over again.

They all had to do with misplaced priorities. Every one of the men regretted "working so hard" at the expense of time with their families. Both men and women wished they'd been more open and honest about their feelings and that they'd made more effort to nurture their relationships with family and friends. Too late, they realized that happiness is a choice—an attitude you can choose to have regardless of your circumstances.

But the number-one regret—at the top of the list—was this: "I wish I'd had the courage to live a life true to myself, not the life others expected of me."[1] Based on what I've experienced in my own life and what I've witnessed in the lives of countless other Christian women—my readers, my sisters, my friends—I'd rephrase it like this: "I wish I had the courage to live a life true to who God created me to be—and that I figured out what that looked like a lot sooner. I wish I had stopped putting so much pressure on myself, and stopped feeling pressured by others to be a woman I never could be, was never meant to be. I wish that I could have just been authentically me. The best version of me. The me Jesus meant me to be."

Instead, too many of us live under constant pressure and stress, worry and fear, guilt and condemnation. We try desperately—and fail miserably (or so it seems)—to measure up to some truly impossible standards, some incredibly unrealistic expectations. We have a vision of what we are supposed to look like, sound like, act like, think like, dress like, work like, rest like, live like, love like . . . an image we've created or been given (or both) that has little connection to reality.

Where does it come from? Where do we get these dreams and visions, these expectations and standards? Why do we feel so much pressure to perform—and conform? I think some of it is external—coming from someone or something outside of us—and some of it is internal. It can come from society, from our culture, from the media. We're constantly being told that we're not "enough." Not tall enough or small enough or thin enough or curvy enough. Not beautiful or sexy enough. Not feminine enough. Not strong enough, not healthy enough. Not smart enough, not kind enough, not important enough. Not educated enough, not artistic or creative enough. Not organized or coordinated or put-together enough. Not diligent enough. Not patient enough, not loving enough, not spiritual enough. Not good enough. Whatever it is, whatever we are, it's not enough.[2]

Sometimes we get the same or similar messages from our friends and family. The expectations they have of us, the standards they hold us to—and the guilt trips they put on us to get us to be and say and do what they want us to do. Though to be perfectly fair, we do the same to them—even when we don't mean to. And some of it is in our heads—it's not really coming from them. Even when it is, we feed into it by refusing to set healthy boundaries. (Jennifer Degler has written a fabulous book on this: *No More Christian Nice Girl: When Just Being Nice—Instead of Good—Hurts You, Your Family, and Your Friends.* See the Recommended Resources for more.)

Some of the pressure comes from our own expectations, our own standards for ourselves. Our own hopes and dreams and imaginations. (I blame all the children's movies of the last thirty years for indoctrinating impressionable young children with the belief that you can be whatever you want to be, as long as you want it badly enough and believe hard enough. I believed *really* hard, and I'm still not graceful or athletic or coordinated enough to be a figure skater or a prima ballerina.)

We don't acknowledge our own God-given individuality, our personalities, our temperaments. Our background and experiences, our strengths and weaknesses. Our learning styles. Our spiritual gifts. All of these things help shape who we are and who we can become. So our lives, our careers, our ministries, our relationships—even our relationships with Jesus!—aren't meant to look like anyone else's. Can't look like anyone else's. They are as unique and individual as we are.

We also don't take into account the season of life we're in. There are all kinds of seasons, and they're constantly changing. Your workload is different when you're launching a business or career or ministry, than when you're maintaining it. The projects you have time to tackle when you have toddlers are different than those you can take on as an empty nester. It's different when you're recovering from trauma, illness, or injury, or when you're caregiving for your elderly parents or your grandchildren. Some things you just can't be (or do) right now—even if you were (or did) before, even if you will again later.

But I think—believe it or not—that of all the sources of pressure, all the places we find ourselves up against what seem like impossible standards, the biggest for us as Christian women is probably our faith. Our understanding (or misunderstanding) of what God expects of us. And how we feel when we fall short before Him.

So many of us feel guilty because we know we're not living as we should. We can't seem to control our tempers or our tongues. We're not nearly as patient, as kind, as loving, as unselfish as we should be. We're not being good stewards of our health, our finances, our time and energy, and our other resources. We don't spend enough time in the Word. We don't pray enough. We don't have faith enough. We're not setting a good example for our children or grandchildren—or for our unsaved coworkers or neighbors or friends. Not being a good witness—not at all. We've just got to find a way to get it together! Or at least make it look like we do.

There are some real problems with projecting the perfect image. First of all, it's simply not true—we are not always happy, optimistic, in command. Second, projecting the flawless image keeps us from reaching people who feel we just wouldn't understand them. And third, even if we could live a life with no conflict, suffering, or mistakes, it would be a shallow existence. The Christian with depth is the person who has failed and learned to live with it.

—Brennan Manning

We've gotten the message that the gospel is all about grace. We know we're not supposed to be desperately trying, constantly striving to earn our salvation, to prove ourselves worthy of God's love and approval. But we don't know how to reconcile that with all the Scriptures that begin "make every effort. . . ."

There are two passages that capture the paradox perfectly. The first is Philippians 2:12–13:

> Therefore, my dear friends, as you have always obeyed—not only in my presence, but now much more in my absence—continue to work out your salvation with fear and trembling, for it is God who works in you to will and to act in order to fulfill his good purpose. (NIV 2011)

And this one, from Ephesians 2:4–10:

> But because of his great love for us, God, who is rich in mercy, made us alive with Christ even when

> we were dead in transgressions . . . in order that in
> the coming ages he might show the incomparable
> riches of his grace, expressed in his kindness to us in
> Christ Jesus. For it is by grace you have been saved,
> through faith—and this is not from yourselves, it is
> the gift of God—not by works, so that no one can
> boast. For we are God's handiwork, created in Christ
> Jesus to do good works, which God prepared in
> advance for us to do. (NIV 2011)

No, we can't earn our salvation. Not even a little. But yes, we do have a part to play. We're supposed to be willing, active participants in the process that leads us to become more and more like Jesus, in the transformation that takes place.

Only God can create in us a new heart, a clean heart. Only He can give us the desire to do right—and enable us and empower us to do it. We have to receive it and believe it.

Here's how Emily Freeman puts it:

> You are not accepted because you are good.
> You are free to be good because you are accepted.
> You are not responsible to have it all together.
> You are free to respond to the One who holds all
>   things in His hands.
> You do not have to live up to impossible
>   expectations.
> You are free to wait expectantly on Jesus, the one
>   who is both the author and perfecter of your
>   faith.[3]

We're not trying to make God love us more. He can never love us more than He already does right now! This very moment. Because His love for us is unconditional. We do good works because He's called us to, created us to, designed us to. We do it out of love for Him, and out of a desire to share His love with others.

The problem is how we respond to failure. How we respond to our human weakness. Our inability to get it all right, every time. Some revert to the kind of legalism that gave us the word "pharisaical." We create an elaborate system of rules designed to regulate our outward behavior, but that does nothing to address the sin in our hearts. If we're successful at keeping these rules, we feel smug and self-satisfied, filled with pride. We look down on other Christians for their "worldliness" or "carnality."

If we find we can't keep these religious rules (our own or those of our church or our family), some of us run to the other extreme: rebellion. It's a rejection, a willful, flagrant flaunting of all those impossible standards and expectations. We give in to sin and rationalize that God is okay with it (calling it grace) or we ignore Him completely.

I think most of us land flat on our faces somewhere in the middle. Sometimes we lean toward legalism, and sometimes we lean toward rebellion. But either way we're leaning, always leaning. Because we're too burdened, too overwhelmed, too exhausted and discouraged and defeated to stand up straight.

It's not really funny. But it does remind me of a cartoon drawn by artist Cathy Guisewite. In the first panel, a woman's hand held up a sparkly ring. The caption read: TO DO: 1955.

There was only one thing on the woman's list—"Marry well." In the second panel, the hand had become a fist. The caption read: TO DO: 1975. Still only one thing, but this time—"Transform the role of women in society!" Then there was TO DO: 1995. The list ran off the page . . . everything from earning a living (in a rewarding career) to marrying and raising a family, taking care of laundry and groceries and bills and cars and pets, fighting fat, toning muscles, rebelling against aging, and—finally—saving the planet!

In the last panel, the Cathy character has collapsed, totally exhausted, on a sofa surrounded with piles and piles of work still to do. She's replaced the cry of the women's liberation movement—"I am woman, hear me roar!"—with "I am woman, hear me snore!"

I know I can relate. Can't you?

There are just not enough hours in the day for all the routine responsibilities of life—let alone our spiritual disciplines, our giving and serving and volunteering. Not to mention our hopes and dreams and plans. For some reason, we're absolutely convinced we really could and should be able to do it all. We tackle our to-do lists with brave and determined faces. But underneath we're stressed. We're anxious. We're worried.

What if we really *can't* do it all? What if we drop the ball? What if we forget something? What if the time or energy or effort we have to give just isn't good enough? What if we fail—fail ourselves, our families, our friends? Our church? Our workplace? What if we fail God? What if we disappoint Him and let Him down? Again.

Remember what Jesus said in Matthew 11:28: "Come to me, all you who are weary and burdened, and I will give you rest." He said He would give us rest. He said His yoke was easy and His burden light . . . meaning the weight of it all would fall on His shoulders, not ours. He promised us freedom—not slavery to sin. And not slavery to a big long list of impossible standards and unrealistic expectations.

God has been reminding me lately that I need only to do the things *He* has given me to do. Not the things I think I should do. Not the things the world tells me I should do, the things our culture or society tells me to do. Not the things people in my industry tell me I should do—or the people in my church or my neighborhood or my community think I should do. Not even the things my friends and family think I should do. Expect that I do. Demand that I do.

Just what Jesus has asked of me. No more and no less.

The secret to "doing it all" is not necessarily doing it all,
but rather discovering which part of the "all"
He has given us to do and doing all of THAT.

—Jill Briscoe

To be honest, it's not always easy to figure out what that means—what it looks like in my life right now. But I know that whatever He asks of me won't be onerous and burdensome, impossible or unreasonable or unrealistic. He's not setting me up to fail. He knows exactly what I'm capable of—what He can and will do, in me and through me. He is patient with me. One thing at a time, one step at a time, one day at a time. Even one hour or one moment at a time. Because He loves me.

He promises to give me all the courage, all the strength, all the wisdom I need, all the direction and guidance I seek (James 1:5). I just have to ask Him!

I really believe that's the key for all of us, right there—for you and for me. To learn to let go of the impossible standards and unrealistic expectations, and even the "perfectly reason-able, perfectly achievable" ones, no matter where they come from or how loudly they clamor for our attention. To let go of all the things that *claim* priority, so we can focus on the things that truly are our priorities—the ones that come from Him.

For some of us, especially, it means learning to let go of our perfectionism. (See pp. 232–235) For all of us, it means growing in grace day by day, learning to walk in freedom. As for those things that we really do need to do, the things we know God is calling us to do . . . well, even if we can't do them perfectly, we keep trying—because He's asked us to.

The wonderful, incredible, miraculous thing is that a fresh start—a clean slate—is only a heartbeat away. Regardless of what we did or didn't do even thirty seconds ago, we can choose to start over right now. This moment. By God's grace and in His strength, we can start anew. We don't have to wait until tomorrow. Or next Monday. Or the next new week, new month, new year. We can ask Jesus to help us right now to do what He wants us to do.

*Run each day's race with all your might so that at the
end you will receive the victory wreath from God. Keep
on running even when you have had a fall. The victory
wreath is won by him who does not stay down, but
always gets up again, grasps the banner of faith and keeps
on running in the assurance that Jesus is Victor!*

—Basilea Schlink

Do the next right thing! It's that simple. Over and over again. No matter how many times we stumble, no matter how many times we fall or fail. As many times as we need a fresh start, there it is!

Oswald Chambers points us to a powerful example of this life-changing truth in Scripture. In a devotional reading called "Taking the Initiative against Despair," Chambers revisits the scene in the Garden of Gethsemane (Matt. 26:36–46). Jesus asked Peter, James, and John to pray. "Then he said to them, 'My soul is overwhelmed with sorrow to the point of death. Stay here and keep watch with me'" (v. 38). But the disciples fell asleep. He awakened them and asked them again to pray—for themselves, for their own sakes, if they couldn't do it for Him. They were going to need it.

Again and again they fell asleep, as He continued to wrestle in prayer, in absolute agony. Alone.

Finally, Jesus came to them and said, "Rise, let us go!"

Talk about feeling like you've disappointed Jesus, like you've really let Him down.

Chambers writes:

The disciples went to sleep when they should have stayed awake, and once they realized what they had done it produced despair. The sense of having done something irreversible tends to make us despair. We say, "Well, it's all over and ruined now; what's the point in trying anymore." If we think this kind of despair is an exception, we are mistaken. It is a very ordinary human experience. Whenever we realize we have not taken advantage of a magnificent opportunity, we are apt to sink into despair.

But Jesus comes and lovingly says to us, in essence, "Sleep on now. That opportunity is lost forever and you can't change that. But get up, and let's go on to the next thing." In other words, let the past sleep, but let it sleep in the sweet embrace of Christ, and let us go on into the invincible future with Him.

There will be experiences like this in each of our lives. We will have times of despair caused by real events in our lives, and we will be unable to lift ourselves out of them. The disciples, in this instance, had done a downright unthinkable thing—they had gone to sleep instead of watching with Jesus. But our Lord came to them, taking the spiritual initiative against their despair, and said, in effect, "Get up, and do the next thing." If we are inspired by God, what is the next thing? It is to trust Him absolutely and to pray on the basis of His redemption.

Never let the sense of past failure defeat your next step.[5]

Let it go. Jesus does. You are never a disappointment to Him.

God loves you unconditionally as you are and not as you should be, because nobody is as they should be.

—Max Lucado

Bible Study

1. Take some time to reflect on the standards and expectations you have for yourself and for others. Make a list (or several, if you need to—what you expect of yourself, what you feel others expect of you, what you yourself expect of your significant others—your family and friends). Then look over the list(s) carefully and prayerfully. Ask God to show you the following.

Where are these standards and expectations coming from?

Are they reasonable? Are they realistic? (Two totally different questions!)

How do I respond when they aren't met?

What does that tell me?

2. Read Luke 10:38–42. It may be very familiar to you, but try to read it with fresh eyes. What is Jesus saying? Put it into your own words.

There are many other Scriptures that talk about priorities—and what "one thing" is needed. It's not the same for everyone. Jesus had different things to say to the Pharisees, for instance, or to the rich young ruler, or to His disciples. It depends on who we are, what our strengths and weaknesses are, what our battles are, what our present circumstances are. But it always starts and ends with honoring God. Obeying God.

Spend some time in prayer, asking God to reveal to you what He wants from you—which of your standards or expectations honor Him, which hopes or dreams or goals you should carry with you, moving forward. And which ones you need to let go.

3. Turn to Isaiah 40:28–31. When you feel worried, weary, or weighed down, what does God promise?

4. Choose one of the following verses—or one mentioned previously in the chapter—to memorize and meditate on this week.

Psalm 46:1	Psalm 29:11
2 Peter 1:5–8	Colossians 2:6–8
Psalm 46:10	2 Corinthians 4:16–18
James 1:2–3	Ephesians 3:20

5. Take a few moments to record any further thoughts or reflections in your journal.

Chapter Four

Holding On to Freedom

My mission in life is not merely to survive, but to thrive, and to do so with some passion, some compassion, some humor, and some style.

—Maya Angelou

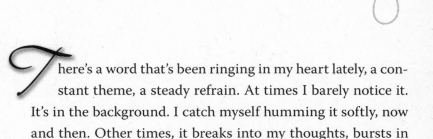

*T*here's a word that's been ringing in my heart lately, a constant theme, a steady refrain. At times I barely notice it. It's in the background. I catch myself humming it softly, now and then. Other times, it breaks into my thoughts, bursts in my ears, drowns out the sound of everything else.

It started when I was working on my book *What Women Should Know about Facing Fear*. I found myself going back in time to some very dark places . . . painful memories of my childhood and early teens. To tell the truth, I had forgotten how dark, how painful those places were—because my life is so different today. I wept as I wrote the word I pray will encourage the countless other women who battle worry and fear: *freedom*.

There is freedom. I am free. You can be free.

Because of Jesus, I'm not the woman I used to be. I'm becoming the woman I was meant to be.

Weeks after I turned in the manuscript, I hit one of those "big" birthdays—one that's hard for a lot of women. It could have been hard for me, too. I could have spent the day reflecting on all the things that didn't turn out the way I'd hoped, the dreams that haven't come true, the things I haven't accomplished or haven't been given. All those great expectations that have given way to disappointment, discouragement, and defeat. (Believe it or not, that's how I "celebrated" my eighteenth birthday. Seriously. I wish I was kidding.)

Instead, I found myself reveling in a fresh vision, a new excitement about this next season of my life and ministry—a sense of anticipation. I can't wait to see what God is going to do!

Free! Free! I am free . . .

"Where the Spirit of the Lord is, there is freedom" (2 Cor. 3:17).

The years have brought with them this unexpected gift. I am free from the angst that characterized so much of my teens and early twenties. I am (mostly) free from the pressure I felt in my late twenties and most of my thirties—the pressure to prove myself, to achieve in my career or my ministry or my personal life what others defined as success. I know who I am now. I'm getting more and more comfortable in my own skin. Not complacent, but content. Confident in my calling. Free.

Not that I don't still have all kinds of other stress and pressure and drama and trauma. My life is full of it. It's part of the human condition. But beneath it all, I find this under-current, this stream that's bubbling up into a noisy, gurgling, irrepressibly joyful spring: *I am free!*

Because of Jesus, I am free.

I'm still a work in progress, but I'm learning every day. I'm growing in His grace. In John 8:31–32, Jesus said if we believe in Him and continue in Him, if we're faithful to His Word, we will know the truth and the truth will set us free.

Then later He said, "I am the truth" (John 14:6).

Though I've never been good at math, even I can grasp this amazing, life-changing equation: know Jesus = know truth = know freedom.

It's something I believe with all my heart that every woman should know.

Learning to walk in the truth, learning to walk in freedom, is a journey. And it takes time. But we keep learning, keep growing, keep moving forward, and eventually we find our way. In this chapter, I want to share with you what I've learned about how to hold on to the freedom knowing Jesus brings—specifically freedom from those impossible standards and unrealistic expectations we talked about in Chapter Three.

Remember who you are. Remember who God made you to be. (If you don't yet know who you are, find out! Set aside some time to prayerfully consider this.) Hold on to the things that make you uniquely, individually, authentically you. Your personality and temperament, your special skills and spiritual gifts and natural talents, your background and experiences, your strengths and weaknesses—all the things that go into making you *you*. Revel in the truth that you are God's masterpiece (Eph. 2:10 NLT). Find your confidence in Him (Ps. 71:5; Jer. 17:7; 2 Cor. 3:4–5).

All those standards you set for yourself, all those expectations—the goals and hopes and dreams—prayerfully revise them to be more in line with the woman you are, the woman God created you to be. Focus on becoming the best version of you that you can be—at this time, in this season of your life. Don't waste another moment wishing you were someone else or pretending to be someone else or trying to make yourself into someone else. And don't let others pressure you, either.

As I was writing this book, Disney introduced its two newest princesses—Anna and Elsa in the movie *Frozen*—and the Academy Award-winning song that took the world by storm: "Let It Go." Talk about serendipity! (My grandmother's favorite word.) Little girls everywhere started singing the song at the top of their lungs, night and day! Some Christian parents immediately expressed concern about the verse that includes the line: "No right, no wrong, no rules for me."[1] Because there are moral absolutes. There is such a thing as right and wrong; there is such a thing as sin and our desperate need for a Savior.

As adults, however, I think we can more readily appreciate the context of the song and the concept that there are things we think of as "right" or "wrong" that really aren't. For instance, we may feel "wrong" because our personalities are different or our gifts and talents are different. We don't fit in—we're not like everybody else. But Jesus has set us free from popularity contests, people pleasing, and peer pressure—even the grownup kind. So we can let it go and be free to be the women He created us to be.

Identify your true priorities. What has God called you to do right now? What are your most important relationships? Responsibilities? Ministries? Tasks or projects? What are the things you genuinely must do? Need to do? Want to do? What are the things that only you can do? Which ones are the most meaningful, rewarding, and fulfilling to you? What kind of season are you in?

It's important to know the answers to these questions, because they help you determine what you do with the time God has given you—what you do with your life, with your time, with your energy. Everything you put on your plate leaves less room for something else. So choose wisely.

Don't say yes to anything out of habit or guilt or obligation. First ask God if it's something He wants you to do. And practice saying no—without offering excuses or explanations that leave us open to arguments or arm-twisting. It's better to simply say, "I'm sorry—I have another commitment." (My commitment is to be faithful to God's call on my life, to be obedient to Him, to take on only the responsibilities He has asked me to, so that I have time for the relationships and ministries He has given me, and to rest and fellowship with Him.)

Learn to set healthier, more reasonable, achievable goals. Identify goals that will actually be helpful to you. Goals that are a part of God's will—His plan and His purpose for you. And learn how to break down those goals into smaller goals—smaller steps that are practical and doable. (You know how to eat an elephant, right? One bite at a time.) It's not necessarily about "lowering" your standards or expectations, but adapting them and adjusting them. There's a lot of trial and error at first. It takes time to find balance. You'll need to figure out what works for you—and what works for you right now, in this season of your life. Maybe some structure and organization would be helpful; then again, maybe you need more freedom, more creativity, more flexibility. Talk to a trusted friend or family member, a godly mentor or accountability partner who can be a good sounding board and offer you some perspective. Most importantly, cover the whole process in prayer.

The wisest choices are made by following the three H's: Listen to your Heart. Use your Head. But, most importantly, follow the leading of the Holy Spirit.
—Georgia Shaffer

Understand that God asks for faithfulness in everything He has called you to, not excellence (1 Cor. 4:2; Gal. 5:22; 1 Pet. 4:10). I'll say it again: faithfulness, not excellence. That's what it really means to do something "as unto the Lord." If you think about it, you know it's not physically possible for you to do every single thing you do each day "excellently"—or even to the best of your ability, every single time. Nor should you. Some things are simply not important enough to deserve more than a minimal amount of your time and effort. Because, again, you only have so much of it. If you're going to walk in freedom, you have to make some choices. You have to set some priorities—based on who you are, and what season of life you're in, and what relationships and responsibilities and ministries God has given you. Be faithful, absolutely. And by all means, be responsible. But give only the important things the very best part of you—the best of your time and talents and energy and efforts. As for the rest, just do the best you can with the time and energy you've got left.

Resist all-or-nothing thinking. This is a tough one for me. My great-grandmother used to sing to me: "There was a little girl who had a little curl right in the middle of her forehead, and when she was good, she was very, very good—and when she was bad, she was horrid!" That about sums it up, right there. I'm still working on recovering or rebounding more quickly when I feel like I've messed up. Reminding myself that my day—or my diet—isn't all ruined by one mistake. Or two or ten. That it's not a reason to give up and throw in the towel. Not if I'm trying to do something God has called me to do. Not if it's important, if it's a goal or a dream, a privilege or a responsibility that comes from Him. A mistake is not a reason to surrender to discouragement or defeat. And it's certainly not a reason to give in to temptation and sin.

Just because I can't do everything I want to do or planned to do—just because I can't do it perfectly or do it on my schedule—doesn't mean I shouldn't do it at all. Doesn't mean I shouldn't do *something*. On my fridge, I have a magnet from First Place 4 Health that reads: "When it comes to exercise, something is better than nothing, and more is better than less." That's true about a lot of things—my devotional life and spiritual disciplines, as well as my big projects, long-term goals, and daily to-dos.

Life does not have to be perfect to be wonderful.
—Annette Funicello

Celebrate your failures as well as your successes. Think of them as learning experiences. Opportunities to gain valuable insight into what works and what doesn't work for you—as well as weaknesses you need to watch out for, areas where you need to grow and improve. It's really true: most of us learn a lot more from our failures than we ever do from our successes. And the things we learn not only benefit us, but they benefit those who come after us—those God has sent us to mentor and minister to. Everyone makes mistakes—it's how you respond to your mistakes that makes the difference.

Part of the problem is the way we define what constitutes "failure" and what constitutes "success." If you've ever been a part of an organized weight loss program, you know the term NSV—non-scale victory. It's learning to look beyond the number on the scale and recognize the growth that's reflected in making good choices, exhibiting positive attitudes and behaviors. Learning to measure progress in a multitude of ways. It's a principle we can—and should—apply to a lot of other areas of our lives.

Don't forget the story of the woman God put in charge of pushing the enormous boulder that blocked the old dirt road. Day after day, sunup to sundown, she pushed with all her might, but the rock was just too huge. It never budged. Not even a millimeter. Still, she kept at it—without any sign of progress (let alone victory)—until God returned, and she collapsed at His feet in a puddle of tears.

"I've been pushing and pushing as hard as I can," she sobbed, "but I just can't move it! I've failed You!"

"You haven't failed Me," He replied. "I didn't ask you to move the boulder. I just asked you to push it. I wanted you to develop the strength, the discipline, the determination, and the endurance that you're going to need for the task I'm giving you next. And you did!"

Watch how you talk to yourself and about yourself. It's one thing to freely admit your failures and mistakes, to be real and honest about your shortcomings, to humbly confess your sins. It's another thing to criticize yourself, berate yourself, belittle yourself, or call yourself names. Jesus doesn't do that to you, and neither should you. It's not helpful, it's not healthy, it's not productive. And most of the time, the things you're saying to yourself aren't true.

I've realized it's not even a good idea to say, "I've been good today" or (alternately) "I've been bad." Because who I am is determined by my relationship with Jesus, not by the choices I've made on any given day. And because that kind of thinking—pronouncing judgment on myself (one way or another)—doesn't benefit me in any way. It's better for me to say "I made good choices" or "I made bad choices," because that puts the emphasis on something I have the ability to control—my choices—rather than my nature. Even better still? Using words like "healthy/unhealthy" or "wise/unwise" reminds me of the significance of my choices and the motivation behind them.

Follow the example of the psalmist (Ps. 42:5, 62:5, 103:2). Replace your negative self-talk with words of truth and grace, hope and faith. Start with Scripture, of course! But you'll also find there are a lot of great Scripture-based quotes and affirmations out there that can help you remember the Truth and apply it to your daily life. Here's something I wrote for myself, combining words and phrases from different Bible verses that God has been speaking to my heart over the past few years. I keep it in my journal and read it from time to time, whenever I feel I'm losing sight of what this journey is about—what the process is for.

> I am becoming a woman of courage,
> a woman of strength, a woman of self-discipline.
> A woman of diligence. A woman of wisdom and
> discernment, a woman of compassion,
> a woman of beauty—true beauty—
> the unfading beauty of a gentle and quiet spirit.
> A woman who loves much,
> because she has been forgiven much.
> A woman of valor who does not run from the battle,
> but to it, fearlessly, relentlessly determined—
> through her obedience—to defeat the enemy and
> bring victory to herself and her people,
> to the glory of God and His eternal kingdom.

It keeps me focused on the Truth, focused on my freedom, rather than my feelings.

Remember whose you are. When you're feeling overwhelmed, stressed out, anxious, and irritable about all the things you're supposed to do, all the things you're expected to do, all the things you can't seem to do—or can't seem to do well or do right—stop and go through your to-do list, asking yourself the following questions:

Why am I doing this?
Who am I trying to please?
What am I trying to prove?

Remember that as you step out onto the stage of life, you are performing for an Audience of One (Gal. 1:10): your Abba Father.

He is the One who created you, who loved you, who called you, who chose you. He is the One who has a plan and a purpose for you—and it's only His plan and purpose that counts. It's only His opinion of you that counts. It's only His approval that matters. No one else's.

He is the One you will stand before, when the curtain finally falls. He is the One to whom you will give an account. He is your Judge. No one else.

"Christ has truly set us free. Now make sure that you stay free . . ." (Gal. 5:1 NLT).

Let go of the impossible standards and unrealistic expectations you have for yourself. Let go of the impossible standards and unrealistic expectations that others try to impose on you—whether they realize they're doing it or not, whether they mean well or not, whether they think they're speaking for Jesus or not.

He can speak for Himself, and you are fully capable of hearing from Him yourself (John 10:1–4). So listen for His voice. And do what He says. Live your life to love Him, honor Him, please Him. And one day, you will hear Him say, "Well done!" (Matt. 25:21).

I live before the Audience of One. Before others I have nothing to prove, nothing to gain, nothing to lose.

—Os Guinness

Bible Study

1. The Bible is full of stories of women who lived for an "Audience of One"—women who did what was right, women who did what God called them to, what God created them to do—no matter what anyone else thought about it. Choose a few to read up on and ask God to teach you something from their examples.

Shiphrah and Puah
(Exod. 1:15–21)

Jochebed
(Exod. 2:1–10; Heb. 11:23)

Miriam (Exod. 2:1–10)

Daughters of Zelophehad
(Num. 27:1–11)

Deborah (Judg. 4–5)

Jael (Judg. 4:17–21)

Ruth (The Book of Ruth)

Abigail (1 Sam. 25)

The Servant Girl
(2 Kings 5:1–3)

Jehosheba (2 Chron.
22:10–12)

Esther (The Book
of Esther)

Elizabeth
(Luke 1:39–45, 57–59)

Mary (Luke 1:26–38)

The Women Disciples
(Luke 8:1–3)

The Syrophoenician Woman (Mark 7:24–30)

The Women at the Foot of the Cross (Matt. 27:55; Mark 15:41; Luke 23:49)

2. Can you think of any other examples? Women from history or from today? Women in the news or women in your own life, whose stories and examples inspire you? What is it about them specifically that speaks to you?

3. Consider creating a motivational board—a poster or journal or scrapbook album (or even a board on Pinterest) where you collect Scriptures, quotes and sayings, and images that speak to you—things that remind you to embrace all that is uniquely you, things that reflect who you truly are and what God has called you to, things that challenge you and motivate you and inspire you.

4. Look up each of the following Scriptural affirmations or declarations. Copy them in the space provided or put them in your own words.

Psalm 73:26	Psalm 119:32
Psalm 139:14	Song of Songs 2:16a
Galatians 2:20	Galatians 5:1
Philippians 3:12	Philippians 3:13–14

5. Try writing your own affirmation, your own declaration, your own definition of freedom—what it looks like for you.

6. Choose one of the verses above—or one mentioned previously in the chapter—to memorize and meditate on this week.

7. Take a few moments to record any further thoughts or reflections in your journal.

Chapter Five

Letting Go of Hurt, Bitterness, and Unforgiveness

It's hard to treat anybody right when our heart isn't right. Even people you want to love may be suffering from your bitterness, resentment, and unforgiveness.

—Joyce Meyer

One Friday morning—years and years ago—I herded my third grade class into the church sanctuary to join the two hundred other elementary school students for our weekly chapel service. As we made our way to our assigned pew, I noticed my friend Dixie—one of the kindergarten teachers—take the stage. It was her turn to share this week.

After pledges and prayers and a few rousing praise songs, the kids settled in and Dixie began with a story about her teenage daughter and a very heavy—much *too* heavy—backpack. Using words even the littlest kids could understand, she told us how the spine isn't designed to carry that much weight, how her daughter had been warned to leave some of her books in her locker or at home, rather than carry them all at once. Dixie demonstrated just how heavy it was, by lifting the backpack and then lifting one of her kindergartners. Clearly, the bag was heavier! There were a few giggles, but they stopped when we all learned that Dixie's daughter had suffered serious damage to her back—she was facing the possibility of surgery and years of physical therapy.

Since every child in the place carried a backpack, Dixie had their attention—as well as that of all the teachers and the moms who'd just happened to stop by. That's when she told us about a different kind of backpack we all carried—an invisible one. And how sometimes it was far more dangerous.

Dixie said she'd seen it with her own kids, in her own classroom. Throughout the day, things happened that hurt their feelings, made them angry or upset them or offended them. They took those feelings and stuffed them in their backpacks. (At this point, she had one of her students join her on stage, carrying an empty backpack. As she gave examples of the kinds of hurts and offenses that the kids could relate to, she put various objects into the bag. As it got heavier and heavier, the tiny kindergartner struggled to stay upright!)

Then Dixie said she'd noticed something else. When the backpack got too full, later that day or maybe the next day, the person carrying it would take something out of it and use it to whack someone else! They might lash out at the person who first hurt them, but then again it might be a totally innocent bystander. She'd realized that their bad behavior may have seemed random, out of the blue—or even out of character. But it wasn't. Instead of dealing with the hurt when it happened— they stuffed it and they carried it until they just couldn't carry it anymore. Then they hurt someone else, who now had something to add to their own backpack.

It was such a simple yet profound illustration of a vital truth: the weight of unforgiveness is crippling—the pain and devastation it causes not only threatens to destroy us, but everyone around us.

Wounded people wound.

As grownups, we see it every day. In the national news, in our local churches and communities, among our own friends and families. In our own hearts. Somehow, we have got to find a way to let it go. Let go of the pain, the hurt, the anger, the bitterness, and the resentment. The unforgiveness. And learn to forgive.

Forgive the slights and snubs and oversights, the misunderstandings. Forgive those who have made us feel unwelcome, unappreciated, unwanted, or unloved. Forgive those who have been impatient or careless or clueless, thoughtless or selfish or cruel or unkind. Forgive the rejection, the abandonment, the abuse, the neglect. Forgive the lies, the deceit, the manipulation, the backstabbing, the betrayal.

Forgive because Jesus said to. And if somehow that doesn't seem reason enough, then because it's killing us not to. When His disciples asked Him to teach them how to pray, Jesus told them to say: "And forgive us our sins, as we forgive those who sin against us" (Luke 11:4 NLT). He also explained, "For if you forgive other people when they sin against you, your heavenly Father will also forgive you. But if you do not forgive others their sins, your Father will not forgive your sins" (Matt. 6:14–15 NIV 2011).

Over and over He made it clear that it's not about how many times someone sins against us or how sorry they are or if they're sorry at all. Or how their sins compare to ours. We are all sinners, in desperate need of God's mercy, in desperate need of His forgiveness and grace. That's the point. That's the deal that He makes. He forgives us our sin against Him, if we forgive others their sin against us.

Frankly, some things are easier to forgive than others. It's easier to forgive when we know that the wound we've suffered, the sin committed against us, was purely unintentional—accidental—or somehow understandable to us. Or when we can tell that the other person is genuinely sorry. Sometimes it's easier to forgive the small stuff—but then again, sometimes it's the small stuff that eats at us.

Not that it really matters which is easier and which is harder. God says to forgive it all.

When you think about it, refusing to forgive rarely hurts the other person. Half the time, they don't even know they hurt us. And if they do, they feel justified in doing whatever they did—so they don't think they need our forgiveness. Even if they do care, even if they truly are sorry, but we aren't convinced—or we don't think they're sorry enough—or that they deserve to be forgiven, no matter how sorry they are—our withholding forgiveness hurts us far more than it could ever hurt them.

As someone once said, holding on to unforgiveness is like drinking poison and waiting for the other person to die.

Unforgiveness is absolutely toxic. It damages us physically, emotionally, and spiritually.

Research has shown it's worse for your health than cigarette smoking! It compromises your immune system, causes high blood pressure, heart attacks, heart disease, tension headaches, teeth grinding, and jaw pain, and it aggravates a host of other medical conditions. It prematurely ages you. (That one right there ought to give you pause!)

Unforgiveness robs you of your peace, your joy, your ability to find meaning and fulfillment in your relationships and your everyday life. Plus, it totally stunts your spiritual growth. It hinders your prayer life a huge way—*huge*. (That distance you feel between you and God—it's not all in your head. See Mark 11:25.)

And it spreads like a cancer, from you to your family to your church family and your friends, to their families and their friends.

> See to it that no one falls short of the grace of God
> and that no bitter root grows up to cause trouble and
> defile many. (Heb. 12:15 NIV 2011)

That's why God is so firm on this, so insistent. He wants us to be well. He wants us to be whole. He wants us to be free. Forgiveness is the only way.

To be a Christian means to forgive the inexcusable,
because God has forgiven the inexcusable in you.

—C. S. Lewis

I think it helps to understand what forgiveness is and what it is not.

Forgiveness is not a feeling. An emotion.

Forgiveness is not ignoring the wrong others have done—pretending it didn't happen or didn't hurt, sweeping it under the rug. It is not minimizing, rationalizing, justifying, excusing, or explaining away sinful behavior.

To forgive someone does not necessarily mean to prevent them from experiencing the fallout—to excuse them or exempt them from the natural consequences of their behavior. (How else will they learn from their mistakes?)

To forgive someone does not necessarily mean to reconcile with them—for the relationship between the two of you to be restored. That might be unsafe or unwise, particularly if the person is unrepentant, or if they say they are sorry but their actions don't reflect a true change of heart. ("The prudent see danger and take refuge"—Prov. 27:12.)

It's important to understand the difference between forgiveness and trust. You can genuinely choose to forgive someone for wrong they have done in the past, without necessarily trusting them to do differently in the future. That's not being suspicious. It's being wise. It's knowing the weakness of human nature, knowing the enemy of our souls and his ability to manipulate and exploit that nature. Trust is something that may or may not come with time.

It's also important to note that when the Bible talks about turning the other cheek, it means not "returning evil for evil." Not retaliating, not being evil and vindictive and vengeful ourselves in response to what others have done to us, but showing His mercy and grace, and in some cases "leaving room for God's wrath"—letting Him settle the score. (See 1 Pet. 3:9, 1 Pet. 2:21–23, and Rom. 12:19.)

It does *not* mean willingly becoming a victim, when there are other options. The call to "patiently endure suffering" is about suffering that is beyond our control, circumstances we cannot escape. It is not about enabling and encouraging others to continually sin against us. The Scripture is very clear about firmly, lovingly confronting sinful behavior (not submitting to it), so that there is at least a possibility that repentance, forgiveness, and reconciliation can take place. (See Matt. 18:15–17, Luke 17:3, and Eph. 4:15.)

Now let's talk about what forgiveness is.

Forgiveness is a choice. A decision.

It's choosing to let go of the hurt, anger, bitterness, and resentment, regardless of what the other person has done, regardless of whether they deserve to be forgiven, regardless of whether they are truly sorry, regardless of whether they apologize, regardless of whether we believe them—if and when they do.

And forgiveness is also a process. A journey. It takes place over time, as we gradually, prayerfully work through a lot of hurt feelings—and then choose to forgive again and again each and every time they resurface.

Forgiveness is relinquishing our right to seek revenge, leaving justice in the hands of God (and in some cases the government or the legal system). Trusting that God sees and He knows, and that He will balance the scales—whether we see it in this lifetime or not.

Forgiveness is believing in God's sovereignty: that nothing happens to us without first passing through His hands of love. That for whatever reason, He allowed this thing to happen, that He was with us when it happened, and that He shares our grief, our pain. That He weeps with us. And that He walks with us through the healing process, through the long journey to forgiveness. That He has some extraordinary things to teach us, some precious gifts to give us, some amazing things He wants to do in us and through us, if we'll let Him.

He promises that He is able to take the most awful, horrible, excruciating, brutally painful things that happen to us—the deepest wounds, the ugliest scars—and turn them into something breathtakingly beautiful.

As Nancy Leigh DeMoss observes, forgiveness is also an act of love and devotion, an act of worship:

> More than an obligation, forgiveness is a high calling—an opportunity to be part of something eternal, to shower back our gratitude to the One who forgave us everything (and you know what that "everything" entails for you). Think of it as an offering, a sacrifice, a love gift to God . . . for Him and Him alone. If He adds to the blessing by causing our forgiveness to be of help to us or others, so much the better. But to know that He is pleased and praised—that is reason and reward enough.[1]

Without forgiveness, there's no future.
—Desmond Tutu

Please understand: I'm not saying forgiveness is easy. It isn't. But whenever I'm tempted to tell God it's too hard—the offense is too great, the wound is too deep—I remember the story of Corrie ten Boom. (I mentioned Corrie in Chapter Two.) Corrie and her sister Betsie were Christians arrested for hiding Jews in their home during the Nazi occupation of Holland. They were sent to a concentration camp in Germany, where they experienced truly unspeakable suffering and torment.

Corrie was later released, and for years afterward, she traveled all over the world, testifying to God's sustaining grace. "There is no pit so deep that the love of God is not deeper still!" One day after speaking at a church service, Corrie came face-to-face with one of her former prison guards. The man had become a Christian, and he wanted to ask her to forgive him for his cruelty at the prison camp. At that moment, all of the awful memories came rushing back in vivid detail.

"My blood seemed to freeze," Corrie said later. "And I stood there and could not. Betsie had died in that place—could he erase her slow terrible death simply for the asking?"

The seconds seemed like hours, as Corrie wrestled with the most difficult thing she ever had to do.

"For I had to do it," she said. "I knew that. The message that God forgives has a prior condition: that we forgive those who have injured us. 'If you do not forgive men their trespasses,' Jesus says, 'neither will your Father in Heaven forgive your trespasses'" (Matt. 6:14–15 KJV).

"Still, I stood there with the coldness clutching my heart. But forgiveness is an act of the will, and the will can function regardless of the temperature of the heart. 'Jesus, help me!' I prayed silently. 'I can lift my hand. I can do that much. You supply the feeling.'"

Suddenly, the healing power of God flooded Corrie's entire being. With tears in her eyes, she cried out, "Brother, I forgive you with all my heart!"

She later exclaimed, "I have never known God's love so intensely as I did then!"[2]

That same healing power that Corrie experienced—the power of God—is available to you and me today. Countless other women have experienced it, too. By His grace, they have let go of their hurt, their bitterness, their unforgiveness. And in return they have received freedom. They have received healing.

Will you?

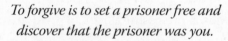

To forgive is to set a prisoner free and discover that the prisoner was you.

—Lewis B. Smedes

Bible Study

1. What have you learned about forgiveness and healing in your own life so far? Have you ever experienced the divine power of God to forgive someone who has significantly wounded you? Have you ever been the recipient of that kind of forgiveness from another person? (Or have you ever witnessed it in your family or church family or circle of friends?)

2. Read Matthew 18:23–35. This teaching is called the Parable of the Unmerciful Servant. What did he do that caused him to be described as "unmerciful"? (v. 30)

Why did Jesus tell this story? What did He want us to understand? (v. 35)

3. Turn to Colossians 3:12–13. What words should describe women who love Jesus? How are we supposed to relate to one another—to the people in our homes, in our families, in our schools, in our workplaces, in our churches, and in our communities?

4. Choose one of the following verses—or one mentioned previously in the chapter—to memorize and meditate on this week.

Psalm 19:12	Psalm 79:9
1 John 2:9	John 13:35
Psalm 32:1	Luke 6:37
1 John 3:14	1 Corinthians 13:4–7

5. Take a few moments to record any further thoughts or reflections in your journal.

Chapter Six

Holding On to Healing

You try to be a model of kindness and love and forgiveness to those all around you, because you have received kindness and love and forgiveness from God through Christ. That's what Christianity is.

—**Patricia Heaton**

*O*ne of the things I love about Corrie ten Boom is her honesty—her transparency. For thirty years after her release from the German concentration camp, the tiny Dutch woman found herself in full-time ministry, as an internationally known author and conference speaker. In her books, Corrie was always very frank about the challenges she faced, the mistakes she made, the sins that had sometimes gotten the better of her.

And believe it or not, the woman who famously forgave one of the Nazi prison guards who had cruelly abused her and her sister still had trouble forgiving other people.

I wish I could say that after a long and fruitful life traveling the world, I had learned to forgive all my enemies. I wish I could say that merciful and charitable thoughts just naturally flowed from me on to others. But they don't. If there's one thing I've learned since I've passed my eightieth birthday, it's that I can't store up good feelings and behavior—but only draw them fresh from God each day.[1]

Corrie wrote these words when she found herself reeling from a nasty exchange with some people who were supposed to be her brothers and sisters in Christ—a disagreement that had led to some unbelievably harsh words directed at her. What further incensed Corrie was that when she ran into these people afterward in a public setting, without ever having apologized, they acted as innocent as lambs—as if nothing had happened between them.

Corrie wasn't fooled. She had forgiven them, of course. But she knew what kind of people they really were. "They forget," she groused to a friend, "that I have it all in writing. I still have those letters they sent me." She had proof.

Corrie's friend said gently, "But aren't you the one who says God has cast all our sin into the depths of the sea?" *Ouch!* And what about 1 Corinthians 13: "Love keeps no record of wrongs . . ."?

Corrie says she couldn't go to sleep that night until she had burned the letters. Holding on to evidence of someone else's sin against her was the same as holding it against them. She was still remembering it and reliving it. Until she let it go, she could not be free of it. She could not experience healing.

Even in her eighties, Corrie was still learning to forgive.

That's what I mean when I say it's a process, a journey. A battle we fight, and keep on fighting.

Because our healing is worth fighting for. Our freedom is worth fighting for.

The good news is that we don't fight this battle alone. God is fighting with us, fighting for us (Ps. 18:30–34; Deut. 3:22, 20:4). And as Corrie pointed out, He has promised to supply all that we need (Phil. 4:19; 2 Cor. 9:8; 2 Pet. 1:3). That includes all the love, mercy, grace, and forgiveness He wants us to receive for ourselves and extend to others.

"He heals the brokenhearted and binds up their wounds" (Ps. 147:3).

I know I still have a lot to learn about letting go of hurt, bitterness, and unforgiveness. But I've had lots of opportunities to practice. And by God's grace—in His strength—I've come a long way. Following are some of the strategies that are helping me fight for—and hold on to—my healing.

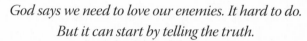

God says we need to love our enemies. It hard to do.
But it can start by telling the truth.

—Viola Davis as Aibileen Clark in *The Help*

Be honest. Start by telling yourself and Jesus the truth. Pour out your heart. Tell the truth about what happened and don't sugarcoat it—call it what it is, or what it was. Tell the truth about how you feel. How you *really* feel. Jesus won't be shocked or horrified, I promise. He already knows. But until you know—until you're honest with Him and with yourself—you can't even begin to heal.

It's really important—when you can—to pray about who to talk to next. (I know, I know—sometimes it all happens so fast!) But when an incident takes place, if it's not a crime, if it's not an act of abuse or violence or harassment—if it's a simple argument or misunderstanding, hurtful as it may be, try to keep it between Jesus and you and the other person. Ideally, you're praying for a swift resolution—healing and forgiveness between you, in which case the less said publicly, the better. There's less chance of the poison of bitterness and unforgiveness spreading to those around you.

But if the situation is a little more complicated, if emotions are running high, if you're not sure what happened or what to think about it or what you should do, it can be really helpful to talk to another person. A spouse, a godly mentor, a trusted friend. We all need perspective sometimes, a sounding board. Someone who can help us determine if we're seeing and thinking clearly. But choose wisely. Choose someone who can listen without judging either of you. Someone who can point you to the Truth. Someone who won't be eager to repeat what you've shared in confidence to others. Someone who wants God's best for you.

It may in fact be a good idea to talk to an experienced counselor (see pp. 236–243), especially if you need someone objective and you're not sure that the people in your life can be—or if there are special circumstances. Maybe you've been the victim of a crime, suffered abuse, or survived some kind of trauma. Maybe you aren't sure whether or not what you've experienced violates the law or constitutes a form of harassment or abuse; there may be other moral or ethical dilemmas. Do you have an obligation to report the incident to the proper authorities? (Who are the proper authorities?) And what would the ramifications be? In addition to helping you process your feelings and emotions, a licensed counselor can help you think through all of these things.

But ultimately, you prayerfully decide what God is leading you to do. Stay in the Word, stay in the Truth. Listen to the Holy Spirit, the Voice of Truth. He will show you.

Be prepared for the battle to take place on many fronts. You've made a decision once and for all to forgive someone for their sin against you just as God in Christ has forgiven you. In one sense, that's it—it's over and done. But in another sense, the battle has just begun!

For one thing, your *feelings* toward the person may or may not change overnight. You may find yourself supernaturally filled with love for them, but you may not. You may find you can feel some pity or some sympathy or some compassion, but you may not. Some days you may battle feelings of anger, bitterness, hatred, or disgust—and battle them you must! Because you don't want those feelings poisoning you. But whether or not you've truly forgiven someone is not about your feelings. How you feel today or tomorrow makes no difference. Feelings come and go. But forgiveness isn't a feeling, it's a choice. And for that matter, so is love. You choose to forgive and you choose to love. That means you choose to see the person the way Jesus sees them—the way He sees you. And you choose to treat them the way He would treat them—the way He treats you. You're going to have to fight your way through some difficult feelings at times, battle some emotional ups and downs. But the forgiveness you've extended to others as an act of obedience to God is still valid, despite the turmoil within.

Then there are the *memories* that will come rushing back to you—and it will be hard not to get caught up in the moment (or moments) time and time again. When you remember a painful incident from the past, it doesn't mean you haven't truly forgiven the person—it means you don't have brain damage. And also that you have an enemy who likes to use your fully functional brain with its fully intact memories to trouble you. What's important is what you do with the memory when it comes— how quickly you choose to change the channel in your head. Quote a Scripture, sing a worship song, spend a few moments in heartfelt prayer—for the person or people involved, or for someone or something totally unrelated. Whatever you think will annoy the enemy of your soul more. (This is war, remember!) Of course, some memories are triggered by consequences of other people's sins against us—consequences we may have to live with every day. It's not easy to walk through that kind of pain. But we don't walk alone. And being reminded of the past or feeling the pain of the past doesn't mean we haven't forgiven the past today.

I'll be honest—the front where I've been defeated most often is in my *thought life*. I get caught all the time "making my case"—rehearsing my grievances, going over and over the story, identifying exactly what someone did that hurt me and how it hurt me and why it hurt me and why it was so unfair, so unjustified, so ungodly, so wrong.

I know I'm not alone in this. Anne Graham Lotz says she struggles with it, too.

> I often rehearse imaginary conversations with my
> wounders, honing my words like knives on flint until
> they are not only sharp, but seem brilliant to me. Of
> course, as my words get sharper and sharper, I find

myself feeling angrier and more justified in self-pity or in plotting revenge. Although I would never speak the words out loud, they shred my inner peace because they keep my focus on "them" and what they did to me. Instead of having an imaginary conversation with myself, I would be better served by pouring out my heart to God in prayer.[2]

Sometimes we're ambushed by our thoughts, our feelings and emotions, our memories . . . we have to fight to take them captive, if we want to experience true healing and lasting peace. But our decision to forgive still stands. And that's something we can rest in, regardless of whether it seems like we're winning or losing the battle on any given day.

Pray for the people who have wounded you (Matt. 5:38–44). Believe it or not, it's one of the best things you can do for you. It proves to you that you truly have forgiven—that you are forgiving—the person. At the same time, it softens your heart and prepares it for the healing work God wants to do. And it protects you from letting any seeds of bitterness or resentment take root.

I've read a lot of books that tell you to pray for your enemies, but not as many that tell you how to pray. Most of them just say "ask God to bless them," and to tell the truth, I've had a hard time with that. Particularly when it comes to praying for those individuals whose sin against me was deliberate and intentional and who are unrepentant—those who continue to sin against others in the same way they sinned against me. How can I ask God to bless the evil they do? Give them all the health, the strength, the energy, the resources they need to keep doing it? Do I pray that He'll send them more victims, more people they can use and abuse? That just can't be right.

But neither is calling down Old Testament vengeance and wrath. It's comforting to read the Psalms—to know I can be real with God and that other people have been where I am and have felt the way I do. But I know what Jesus said. So what do I do?

What's helped me the most is to pray for my enemies the way I would pray for myself. Or the way I would pray for someone I really loved, who was headed down the wrong road.

Pray that God really gets hold of their heart, and that they come to know Jesus, if they don't already. That they really and truly experience His love for them. That they see the mistakes they're making, the hurt they're causing, the wrong they're doing. That they have a heart to repent and turn around and head in the right direction. That they hear His voice and know His Truth. That they experience His forgiveness and mercy and grace—and that they extend it to others. That they find hope and healing. That God gives them the courage and strength to walk in obedience to Him and shows them what to do. That He blesses their efforts to honor Him, big and small.

These are the kind of things I want for myself and for the people I love. They are the kind of blessings I can pray for anyone.

You will know that forgiveness has begun when you recall those who hurt you and feel the power to wish them well.

—Lewis B. Smedes

Remember that Jesus isn't asking you to do anything He didn't already do. Remember what He went through. "He came into the very world he created, but the world didn't recognize him. He came to his own people, and even they rejected him" (John 1:10–11 NLT). During His time on this earth, the Lord Jesus was constantly made the subject of gossip and rumor and innuendo. He was lied about and lied to. When He started His public ministry, His own family tried to stop Him, because they thought He was out of His mind (Mark 3:21). His actions were questioned, His methods were questioned, His motives were questioned, His theology was questioned, His authority was questioned. Everything He said, everything He did, everywhere He went, everyone He talked to—His whole life put under a microscope and subjected to others' judgment and criticism. He was routinely cursed, yelled at, spat upon, mocked, and ridiculed. Harassed, verbally and physically attacked, plotted against and falsely accused. In the end, He was betrayed by those closest to Him. Betrayed and abandoned by those He had poured His life into. And what about all the thousands of people He ministered to? All the thousands He fed? All the ones He healed and delivered? Were they in the crowd, shouting "Crucify him!" as the soldiers whipped His back to shreds and pressed the crown of thorns on His head?

It's not just the brutal, agonizing death on the cross that He suffered, but everything it took to get there. The Bible tells us He endured it all "for the joy set before Him"—the joy of being able to lay down His life for us, so that He could forgive us and be reconciled to us forever.

So nothing He asks of you, nothing He asks of me, is too much. Whatever we have to endure. Whatever we have to forgive. We can do it, because He did.

By Your grace, in Your strength, for Your glory, Lord Jesus— and for love of You.

Redeem the pain of the past by making it serve you in the future. You do this by letting it teach you, on a lot of different levels. For example, instead of becoming bitter by being absorbed in your own pain, you become more sensitive to other people's pain—more caring and compassionate. More Christlike. Once you know—on any level—what it feels like to be hurt, to be rejected, to be abandoned, to be neglected, and to be mistreated, misjudged, or misunderstood—you can use that pain to connect with others. Even if your experiences are different, the feelings are the same. It suddenly adds a whole new depth and dimension to your ministry—the "fellowship" of suffering. "Praise be to the God and Father of our Lord Jesus Christ, the Father of compassion and the God of all comfort, who comforts us in all our troubles, so that we can comfort those in any trouble with the comfort we ourselves have received from God" (2 Cor. 1:3–4).

You can also learn a lot about the kind of person you want to be—and the kind of person you don't want to be—from the way other people have been with you. Some of the kindest, most considerate, most thoughtful people I know are the people who've been wounded and learned to think about what they say before they say it or think about what they do before they do it. They think about how it might affect you because they know what it's like to be hurt, to be crushed, to be devastated.

They don't want to put anyone else through the things they've been through. And they've become better for it.

Finally, with some time and distance, you may find you can more objectively evaluate some of the hurtful things that have happened to you—and discover some things that will ultimately benefit you. For example, in some cases, I've come to realize that I was just as guilty as the other person. We hurt each other; we were both to blame. If I want to have a clear conscience before God, if I want to learn and grow and mature as a human being, if I want to have healthy relationships moving forward, then I have to learn to take responsibility for my part and the choices that I made.

In other cases, I know now that—while it wasn't technically my fault—I could have handled things differently. I could have chosen my words more carefully, or been more patient, sympathetic, or understanding, or been less quick to judge.

In still others, I see that the enemy of my soul set a trap for me—and used another person to do it. I was an innocent victim, but there were certain things that made me particularly vulnerable, things that made me uniquely susceptible. Perhaps it was in my need for approval or affirmation or some similar desire. Some weak spot or personal issue I wrestle with. Seeing how the enemy targeted that weakness—how and why I fell into that trap—that's *very* valuable information to me.

In some cases, there were warning signs—lots of red flags waving wildly—that at the time (I can admit now) I pretended I didn't see.

And other events totally blindsided me.

Just to be clear, learning from the past is not about blaming the victim. I am responsible for my sins. They are responsible for their sins. And sometimes whether I could have or should have known better / seen it coming / done something to prevent it is a moot (and not particularly helpful) point. But I've found I can learn things that will help me and help me help others. It feels good to get something positive out of those painful experiences!

Be prepared for the possibility of one of several different outcomes. Sometimes there is no justice this side of eternity. And no resolution, no closure—let alone restoration or reconciliation. It's just not possible. The other person may have died—or they may be living, but you may not know where to find them. They may be thoroughly unrepentant, unwilling to even acknowledge what they've done or hear your side. They may be unsafe or unstable—totally incapable of having a rational conversation, but fully capable of causing you more harm. I've been in a few situations like this. It's so hard. I've learned that all I can do is focus on my part, in my own heart.

"But if you suffer for doing good and you endure it, this is commendable before God. To this you were called, because Christ suffered for you, leaving you an example, that you should follow in his steps.... When they hurled their insults at him, he did not retaliate; when he suffered, he made no threats. Instead, he entrusted himself to him who judges justly" (1 Pet. 2:20–23).

There will come a day. God sees. God knows.

Sometimes you can actually get closure. You can get resolution. There may not be much relationship moving forward, but maybe there wasn't much to begin with. Or maybe with everything that's happened, you realize it can never be the same. But at least the wrong is acknowledged and addressed. Apologies are made. Perhaps even genuine, heartfelt apologies. Forgiveness is asked for and received. Enough said. I've experienced this kind of outcome, too. It's better, a lot better. But it's not as good as it gets.

Sometimes—sometimes—there is the incredible, miraculous, supernatural intervention of God. A couple of broken, mixed-up, messed-up people humble themselves before Him and before each other. And they experience His divine power to forgive.

Deeply, truly, freely.

The forgiveness is flowing. The love is flowing. The mercy is flowing. The grace is flowing. The tears are flowing. Boy, are they flowing!

And the healing begins. There may have been a series of trembling, hesitant steps leading up to this point—and a series of cautious, careful steps afterward. But the point is, the relationship not only survives but thrives. It's stronger than ever.

That's restoration and reconciliation, and I've experienced it, too. I know it's possible. It does happen. I hear others share their own amazing stories—their testimonies—of divine forgiveness, healing, and restoration every day.

In the meantime, focus on what you've gained or been given or have left—not on what you've lost. It sounds trite, but it's true: one of the best things you can do is to count your blessings. In everything, give thanks. Find little things to celebrate, things that make you laugh or bring you joy, things that help you take your mind off your pain and remind you that life is still a beautiful thing. There are still some pretty wonderful (if imperfect) people that the love of Jesus shines through. Be determined to look for the good in others and believe the best. Light a candle, rather than cursing the darkness. Or, as Romans 12:21 puts it, "Do not be overcome by evil, but overcome evil with good."

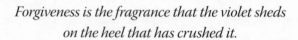

Forgiveness is the fragrance that the violet sheds
on the heel that has crushed it.

—George Roemisch

On the wall of her children's home in Calcutta, India, Mother Teresa had posted a version of the Paradoxical Commandments, originally created by Christian author and speaker Dr. Keith M. Kent.

People are often unreasonable,
irrational, and self-centered.
Love them anyway.
If you are kind, people may accuse you
of selfish, ulterior motives.
Be kind anyway.
If you are successful, you will win some unfaithful
friends and some genuine enemies.
Succeed anyway.
The good you do today will be forgotten tomorrow.
Do good anyway.
If you are honest and sincere people may deceive you.
Be honest and sincere anyway.

What you spend years building could be
destroyed overnight.
Build anyway.
People really need help, but may attack you
if you help them.
Help them anyway.
Give the world the best you've got, and you'll
get kicked in the teeth.
Give the world the best you've got anyway.[3]

Don't let your wounds turn you into a person you are not. Stay true to the woman God created you to be. Walk in mercy and grace, forgiveness and freedom. Hold on tight to your healing!

Bible Study

1. Take some time to pray and ask God to show you if there is any hurt or bitterness or unforgiveness in your heart—anyone you have not yet forgiven. Write down any specific names or incidents that come to mind. One by one, go down the list. Confess any sin or wrongdoing on your part, make the decision to forgive the person and release them to the Lord, then pray for them.

If you find a particular person or incident that you just cannot bring yourself to forgive, ask God to help you—to work in your heart to overcome whatever is holding you back and keeping you from obeying Him in this. And pray about seeing a counselor or talking things over with a trusted friend.

2. Ask God to show you if there is anyone you have wronged that you have yet to ask for forgiveness (Matt. 5:23–24). And

pray about how to go about apologizing to them. Depending on the nature of the offense and the relationship you have with the person, it may be more appropriate to call them or e-mail them or ask them out to coffee—or catch them in the kitchen before they head to work or school!

3. Look up the following Scripture passages:
   a) Genesis 16:1–14: What did Hagar discover about God when she felt used and abused and utterly alone? (v. 13)

   b) Genesis 29:31–35: Where did Leah learn to turn, when she experienced nothing but rejection from her husband, her sister, and her family? (v. 35)

c) Genesis 50:20: What did Joseph say about being betrayed by his own brothers, sold into slavery in Egypt, falsely accused of sexual assault, and imprisoned for three years?

4. Choose one of the following verses—or one mentioned previously in the chapter—to memorize and meditate on this week.

Psalm 56:8   Psalm 30:2

Isaiah 12:2   Psalm 62:7

Psalm 34:18   Jeremiah 17:7

Psalm 18:2   Psalm 3:3

5. Take a few moments to record any further thoughts or reflections in your journal.

Chapter Seven

Letting Go of the Illusion of Control

[My dad] would get these far-off looks in his eyes and he would say, "Life doesn't always turn out the way you plan." I just wish I'd realized at the time, he was talking about my life.

—Sandra Bullock, as Lucy in *While You Were Sleeping*

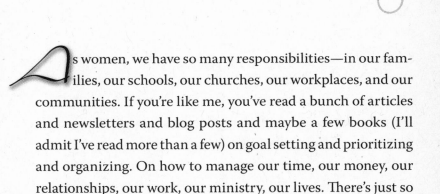

As women, we have so many responsibilities—in our families, our schools, our churches, our workplaces, and our communities. If you're like me, you've read a bunch of articles and newsletters and blog posts and maybe a few books (I'll admit I've read more than a few) on goal setting and prioritizing and organizing. On how to manage our time, our money, our relationships, our work, our ministry, our lives. There's just so much to do. Anything that helps make it simpler or easier, right?

It turns out there's a lot we can learn, a lot we can do. There are all kinds of choices we can make. There are things we can control—our own attitudes, for instance, and the actions we take. But sometimes we get the wrong message. We come away with the impression (one we're all too susceptible to) that it is possible to control almost everything. Everything that matters, that is. We just need the right tools, the right tips, the right techniques.

It's a huge temptation we face, the temptation to live our lives in an endless quest for control—or the illusion of control.

It's a desperate desire. An aching need.

We get it from our Mother—the Mother of all the Living—Eve.

It started in Eden, during what seemed like an innocent conversation, with what sounded like an innocent question. The serpent asked Eve, "Did God really say, 'You must not eat from any tree in the Garden?'"

But the serpent was crafty—more crafty than any of the creatures God had made. The whole thing was a setup. A carefully constructed trap. Eve obligingly explained God's command and the consequence of eating from the tree of the knowledge of good and evil. But the serpent contradicted her. "You will not surely die," he hissed. "For God knows that when you eat of it, your eyes will be opened, and you will be like God, knowing good and evil" (Gen. 3:4–5).

Think about what the serpent was really saying here: What God says is wrong. God lies—or at least misleads us. He can't be trusted. And God deliberately withholds good from His children out of spite. In other words, "God knows this is really wonderful, and He just doesn't want you to have it." The accusation is that God is unjust and unfair and unkind.

If this is true, then Eve has no reason to believe Him, no reason to trust Him, no reason to obey Him. Why shouldn't she take control of her own life?

Eve listened to the serpent that day—she believed him instead of God. So she disobeyed God—she rebelled against God. She believed, in her naiveté, that she would have control now. Only to find that she didn't have control at all—the serpent did. Her newly sin-stained, corrupted nature did.

Over the years, Satan's strategy hasn't changed much. He whispers the same things to our hearts today. He takes any and every opportunity to malign the character of God and undermine our faith in Him. In John 8:44, Jesus said the devil "was a murderer from the beginning, not holding to the truth, for there is no truth in him. When he lies, he speaks his native language, for he is a liar and the father of lies."

He tries to convince us that we need control, we want control, we must have control. Of course, we don't take much convincing, because we were born with that birth defect—that sin nature—already in us. Thanks, Mom.

Sometimes the root of it is stubbornness, arrogance, or pride. But I think more often it's fear. As women, one of our greatest needs is for security. We want to feel safe. We want to *be* safe. We want the people we love to be safe. And happy and healthy. We want the world to be a safe and happy place.

But it isn't always.

That doesn't keep us from doing our level best—anything and everything we can think of. We worry that we might not be able to stay on top of all our responsibilities. It takes a lot of effort to keep it all together, keep things running smoothly. We worry that others will somehow see—or even suffer from—our faults and failures and shortcomings. We're afraid we might lose control over dozens of things that—in reality—we have no real control over anyway.

We're afraid things won't turn out the way we want them to, the way we think they should. We try to take charge. We try to take over. We want to fix things. We want to fix people. So we take them into our own hands—instead of trusting them to God.

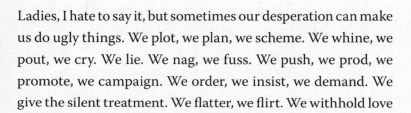

Fear arises when we imagine that
everything depends on us.
—Elisabeth Elliot

Ladies, I hate to say it, but sometimes our desperation can make us do ugly things. We plot, we plan, we scheme. We whine, we pout, we cry. We lie. We nag, we fuss. We push, we prod, we promote, we campaign. We order, we insist, we demand. We give the silent treatment. We flatter, we flirt. We withhold love and affection or approval. Whatever it takes! We tell ourselves it's necessary. We have to do it this way.

The trouble is that our attempts to control the uncontrollable inevitably backfire. All our efforts only leave us feeling irritable, upset, stressed, and miserable. It's not easy trying to run the world! People just won't cooperate. Circumstances won't cooperate. Life won't cooperate. Why can't everybody get with the program? Eventually we're exhausted, weary, and worn out.

When we're finally forced to accept the reality that there are—in fact—things we can't control, some of us turn to the dark side. Okay, the dark(er) side. We focus with renewed energy and zeal on whatever it is that we actually can control. We make epic battles out of things like the "right way" and the "wrong way" to load the dishwasher or fold the towels or hang the toilet paper. (Which way is the right way? Our way, of course.) Seriously, it can manifest in perfectionism or obsessive-compulsive behavior.

The more controlling, the more uncompromising, the more inflexible we become . . . the more we risk damaging or even destroying our relationships with others. They don't like being told what to do all the time, feeling constantly criticized, corrected, coerced, micromanaged, and manipulated.

It's hard for us to see it at the time, when we're in the middle of it. Because we're usually convinced that our motives are good. Our intentions are good. We believe we have others' best interests at heart. We don't mean to hurt or offend or alienate anyone. But we do. We just can't help ourselves.

When we're so intent on making our hopes, our dreams, our visions—for ourselves or for others—come true, we can't see what God wants to do. When we're so driven by our plans, our agendas, we risk running out ahead of Him, resisting His will, or missing it entirely. Instead of working with Him to accomplish His purposes for us and the people we love, we just get in the way. We cause ourselves all kinds of heartache and pain. We create unnecessary problems and delays.

God always gives His best to those
who leave the choice with Him.

—Jim Elliot

Let's take a look at the examples of four of the most famous women in the Old Testament. Their stories are probably familiar to you, so I'll just summarize the relevant points here.

Sarah: God had promised to make her husband Abraham "the father of many nations" and give the land of Canaan to their numerous descendants. But when years passed (too many, Sarah thought) and she was far too old to get pregnant, Sarah came up with a plan. She gave her maidservant Hagar to Abraham, so that the younger woman could bear him a son. Which she did. Then, fourteen years later, at the age of ninety, Sarah got pregnant herself with Abraham's heir—just as God had said. (Genesis 16:1–15, 18:1–15, 21:1–20)

Rebekah: God told Rebekah while she was still pregnant that when her babies were born, "the older would serve the younger"—that her younger son, Jacob, would inherit the favor and blessing of God (in addition to his family's prominence, prestige, and wealth) contrary to cultural tradition. Years passed, and Rebekah came up with a plan to deceive her husband into giving the blessing to Jacob, her favorite. Which he did. But then Jacob had to run for his life when his brother threatened to kill him. And though he did indeed become a blessed man, his mother never saw him again. (Genesis 25:23, 27:1–13)

Abigail: Everyone knew that the mighty warrior David was God's anointed and Israel's next king. So when Abigail heard that her husband Nabal had foolishly insulted him and provoked him to war—a personal, private war on her household—she came up with a plan. She rode out to meet David and his army, with gifts of food and drink. As she apologized for her husband's behavior, she spoke with such truth, such grace, such wisdom, that she melted the heart of the future king. And when her husband died, David wasted no time in making her his wife (1 Sam. 25).

Naomi: After her husband died, after her sons died, the widow Naomi returned to her old hometown with her faithful daughter-in-law, now a widow, too. They had no money, so

Ruth went to work in the fields to support them, but it wasn't a long-term solution. When Naomi discovered that the kind and generous owner of the fields had taken notice of Ruth—that of all things he was single (!) and a distant relative with an obligation to the family—Naomi came up with a plan. She gave Ruth step-by-step instructions to secure a marriage proposal—which she did. And the happy couple became a part of Jesus' family tree. (Ruth 3:1–18)

When you look at their stories, you see that all four of these women were strong, courageous, determined women. All four wanted what was best for their families—all four thought they knew what was best for their families. All four thought they knew God's will for their families—two of them even had prophetic words to go on. All four were ready and willing to do whatever they needed to do to make it happen. And all four of them did—in fact—make plans and take strategic action. But only two of them got it right.

Only two of them (Abigail and Naomi) were being led by God, doing as He directed them. The other two (Sarah and Rebekah) were running ahead of Him, doing what seemed best to them.

On the surface, their choices seem so similar.

But there's a difference between doing the will of God and doing what we will. Acting out of obedience to Him and acting without regard for Him. Serving under His command and trying to take control—trying to manipulate things to make them turn out the way we want them to. (For all the right reasons, with the best of intentions, even thinking we have His blessing—of course!)

And we're more likely to err in one direction than the other. I mean, honestly, in twenty-five years of women's ministry, I've never heard another woman say, "See, my problem is I spend *too* much time making sure it's *God's* will I'm seeking, and not my own. . . ." (Nor, I hasten to add, have those words ever crossed my lips.)

It's true that in spite of the terrible mistakes Sarah and Rebekah made, God still accomplished His purposes for them and for their families and for all of humanity. But it was so much more difficult, so much more painful than it had to be. They suffered for it. Generations of their family suffered for it. The whole world has suffered for it. It's the original source of the continuing war and conflict in the Middle East.

So if you have a choice (and you do), why would you choose the hard way? Choosing to surrender—to "let go and let God" may seem like the hard way at first, but not if you take the long view.

I think that's our challenge, really, to be strong, determined, courageous women of God who answer His call and take action in our own lives or on behalf of our families or for His kingdom—in His time, in His wisdom, in His strength, at His direction, in His way! To do it without running out ahead of Him, taking on assignments He hasn't given us, fighting battles that aren't ours to fight, breaking off to pursue our own agenda or pursue His agenda in our own time, our own wisdom, our own strength, our own way.

We've got to learn to trust Him and His leadership. Trust Him and His power. Trust Him and His wisdom. Trust Him and His love. It's because we trust Him—trust that He is in control—that we can let go.

For most of us the prayer in Gethsemane is the only model. Removing mountains can wait.

—C. S. Lewis

Years ago, I remember attending a professional women's conference. I was smiling cheerfully on the outside, but on the inside I felt like I was falling apart. Everything in my life seemed like it was spinning wildly out of control. I'd been working hard to get it together—keep it together—but I just couldn't do it.

I hated to admit it, but the things that were weighing on me were beyond my power to control. They'd never been in my power in the first place. There was nothing I could do—at least nothing in my own wisdom, in my own strength, nothing I could see. But that hadn't kept me from trying. Now here I was, frustrated and upset, anxious and worried and worn out from all the fruitless effort.

Then a woman I'm honored to call my friend, Jennifer Kennedy Dean, took the platform. She told a story about a time she went to an outdoor market with one of her young sons. Someone gave him one of those big, beautiful helium balloons tied to a string. She told him more than once to hold on tight. (You know what happens with little children and balloons.)

But despite her warnings, sure enough, the next time she turned around, her little boy was searching the sky for a last glimpse of his precious balloon. Anticipating tears or a tantrum, she scolded him, "Honey, I *told* you to hold on tight! Why did you let it go?"

Her toddler replied, "I didn't let it go, Mommy! I gave it to Jesus."

It made me cry.

Because . . . well, what a sweetheart! And that's it right there, isn't it? The answer. For me and for you. There are so many things we just can't control. The answer is "let it go." But the only way we can really let it go is if we're giving it to Jesus. Because we don't want to walk away from the things that are important to us. The people who are important to us. All of our responsibilities. We don't want to ignore them or neglect them or give up on them. That's not what "letting it go" means.

We're not abandoning them. We're entrusting them to the Creator of All Things. To the One who is so much wiser, so much stronger, so much more resourceful, so much more just and good and patient and loving and kind. He knows what to do, so much better than we do.

Sometimes when we step back and take a deep breath, He'll unfold a little of His plan—He'll give us a task, something He wants us to pray or say or do. Other times He'll show us that He can take care of it Himself, without our help.

But either way, the difference it makes is huge! It's hard to describe the relief, the peace, the freedom.

And when that temptation comes again—the temptation to try to control what you can't control?

Let it go!

Give it to Him.

Bible Study

1. Do you have a hard time letting go of things that you really can't control? What things? Which people? Which circumstances? Are there specific areas of your life where it's harder than others? Why do you think that is?

For now, make a list of things you can't control and need to let go of—the people, the problems, the circumstances. Begin praying over them, asking God to help you release them to Him. With Jennifer's story in mind, you might also:

- Write the names or key words in marker on a helium balloon and pray over it as you take it outside, let it go, and "give it to Jesus."
- In your journal, draw balloon shapes (or use a stencil or scrapbooking supplies to cut and glue colorful balloons) and label them with the names and descriptions of things you're giving to Jesus. Whenever you're tempted to take them back, turn to that page, place your hand over them and "release them" again and again.

2. Sometimes when we pray, we're really just telling God what we think He should do—or what we want Him to do. There are a lot of problems with this approach to prayer, not the least of which is that when we're at a loss—when we don't know what we want or what to tell Him—we don't come to Him at all. Turn to 2 Chronicles 20. What crisis did King Jehoshaphat and the people of Judah face? (vv. 1–2)

What did they do? (vv. 3–4)

What did King Jehoshaphat pray? (v. 12)

What did God say? (vv. 15–17)

To find out what happened—it was incredible!—see verses 21–25. Ask God to show you if there's a situation in your life today that could use this same kind of prayer—this same kind of battle strategy.

3. Choose one of the following verses—or one mentioned previously in the chapter—to memorize and meditate on this week.

Isaiah 55:8–9   Proverbs 3:5–6

Psalm 143:8–10   Psalm 91:1

Psalm 25:4–5   Psalm 40:8

James 1:5   Psalm 44:3

4. Take a few moments to record any further thoughts or reflections in your journal.

Chapter Eight

Holding On to Peace

*Ox: "You work hard, try to provide for the family,
and then, for one minute, everything's good.
Everyone's well. Everyone's happy.
In that one minute, you have peace."*
Jack: "Pop, this isn't that minute."

—While You Were Sleeping

In 2005, *American Idol* winner Carrie Underwood released a song that raced to the top of the *Billboard* charts, winning multiple Grammy Awards, Country Music Awards, Gospel Music Awards, and many more. "Jesus, Take the Wheel" would go on to sell over two million copies. In the first year alone, more than a million people made it their cell phone ringtone.

It's not hard to understand the appeal of the song—it's not just because it's sung by a fan favorite, a beautiful and talented star. It's because it's a song with a message. It tells a story we can all relate to.

A young woman is driving down the road after a snowstorm, with her baby in the backseat of the car. When she hits a patch of black ice, she loses control of the car and realizes they're going to crash and die. So she cries out to God in prayer—and their lives are miraculously spared.

Afterward, as she's sitting by the side of the road, she realizes that—just like her car had been moments ago—her life is spiraling out of control. She's made poor choices. She's taken the wrong road. And she knows she is powerless to save herself, so she prays that Jesus will "take the wheel" and turn her heart and life around.[1]

I think we've all had moments when we felt our lives were crashing down around us. When everything seemed completely out of control. We remember the desperation, the helplessness, the hopelessness.

And we remember more. We remember Jesus coming to our rescue, as He has time and again. As we admitted how foolish we'd been and how much we needed Him. How He didn't condemn us, didn't lecture us, didn't criticize us. He just loved us and saved us. And steered us out of the ditch. Back on the road. The right road.

What a sweet relief it was—it is—to let Him take the wheel. To know that He was in control. He would take over from here. The trouble is, after a while, we start inching back over into the driver's seat. Sliding our hand up on the steering wheel. We really think it would be better to take *this* road. . . . We're not sure where's He's taking us. We don't know what lies ahead. We think we'd feel better in the driver's seat. So we take back the wheel. And just like that, we forfeit our peace.

Because Jesus doesn't just give us peace. He is our peace (Eph. 2:14).

So when we push Him out of the way, we push away our peace.

God cannot give us a happiness and peace apart from Himself because it is not there. There is no such thing.

—C. S. Lewis

The way we hold on to our peace is to hold on to Jesus. And let Him hold on to the wheel—let Him take the wheel—every single day. Whether there's been a snowstorm lately or not. Whether we see black ice or not.

Ask Jesus to take the wheel even when the sun is shining and the road is clear. Even when we're feeling good, feeling strong, feeling like we've got this. Even when we think we know the route.

Truthfully, it's easier to pray "Jesus, take the wheel" when we don't have any other options. When it's that, or end up in a ditch. Or when we're already in the ditch and He's the only way out. But going from ditch to ditch is a lousy way to drive. A lousy way to live.

We really don't have to wait to see our lives flashing before our eyes before we surrender to Him. It's actually better not to wait! Surrender before, and it's amazing how many of those ditches disappear. Moment by moment, hour by hour, day by day, our prayer needs to be the prayer of Jesus in Gethsemane: "Not My will, but Thine be done."

That's the real secret of serenity—surrender. That's how we hold on to peace—by placing our trust in the person of Jesus.

These are some of the things I've learned—practical, purposeful things we can do to help us hold on to Jesus, hold on to our peace. Things that will help us cultivate a peaceful spirit.

Remember to make time to be alone with Jesus—to reconnect with Him. And think of that time as a "spa for your soul." My friend Cindy McDowell explains that a spiritual spa is "taking time to relax in the presence of our loving God, to reflect on His goodness and His gifts, to talk to Him about all that concerns us and, more importantly, to listen carefully to that still small voice."[2] Jesus Himself frequently took time away to pray, to rest in His Father's embrace. (See, for instance, Matt. 14:23, Mark 1:35, Mark 14:32, Luke 9:18, and Luke 11:1.) It's not every time that you have a deeply moving, "mountaintop" experience. But if your time with Him is consistently dull, dry, and boring—if it's difficult and laborious—then you're doing it wrong. Wrong for you, that is. It's not one-size-fits-all.

Biblically speaking, there's no correct or incorrect way to have a quiet time, no scripturally determined process or formula. It's not in the Bible. I've checked. So experiment with different settings (indoor, outdoor, curled up with a cozy blanket—or not, if it makes you sleepy!) and different times of day. Try using a really structured, in-depth Bible study—or try a less structured, more spontaneous approach. If you're an artist, draw while you pray. If you're a musician, play or sing. And even if you're not! Light candles or wear a prayer shawl if you understand the tradition and history, and if the symbolism is rich and meaningful to you. Your quiet time can be really quiet, if that's how you like it. Or really lively and energetic, if that's how you are. Because *of course* your God-given personality and temperament influence your relationship with Him—how could they not?

So pay attention to what you're doing when you feel closest to Him, the times and places and ways you most often hear from Him—and look for ways to incorporate elements of those things into your regular routine. (If this idea is new to you, you might enjoy Betty Southard's book *Come as You Are: How Your Personality Shapes Your Relationship with God*.) Again, think "spa for the soul"—or, better yet, "date with the ultimate love of my life." Ask yourself: "How can I make our time together special?" I know it may seem like one more thing on your to-do list, but if you get this right . . . if you actually look forward to and enjoy spending time with Jesus, if you're actively learning and growing in your relationship with Him, you have peace. And so many other things just fall into place—or into perspective. They really do.

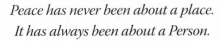

Peace has never been about a place.
It has always been about a Person.

—Jennifer Dukes Lee

Remember the power of praise and worship to bring peace to your soul. The Scriptures tell us that when David played his psalms, the demon that tormented King Saul fell silent. The anger, the fear, the confusion, and the paranoia with which it had filled his heart dissipated, and the evil spirit left him (1 Sam. 16:14–23). I know when my own spirit is under attack—if I sing songs about the blood of Jesus that was shed for me, and the victory that He won on Calvary—if I put praise and worship music on in the house or the car or my iPod, the atmosphere instantly changes. Sometimes I choose soft, soothing music . . . beautiful hymns or reverent instrumental collections. Sometimes I listen to the upbeat contemporary Christian music I loved when I first gave my heart to Jesus as a teenager. It brings back so many memories—so many things He's brought me through! Then there are times when I need some stirring praise anthems. And declarations of war.

When you think about it, praise and worship is one of our most powerful weapons against the enemy of our souls. Over and over in the Old Testament, God sent His armies into battle with little more than a song of praise on their lips. And that praise was the key to their victory. With a mighty shout, the walls of Jericho fell down (Josh. 6:20). Incredibly, it was often the choir that led the charge. When the people sang God's praises, their enemies fell into confusion and defeated themselves (2 Chron. 20:22). By praising God in the midst of his suffering, Job proved that his heart was true—that he loved God and not just His gifts, at the same time giving the devil (who had said otherwise) a black eye (Job 1:1–2:10). A kick in the gut. That's what our praise has the power to do. Considering all the misery the devil has caused, I'm not at all sorry about that. In fact, it gives me great satisfaction. I wish I remembered to praise God more often, just for that very reason. Defeating the enemy—that's another way to hold on to your peace.

Remember to pray—even before all else fails. Preferably _long_ before all else fails. "Give all your worries and cares to God, for he cares about you" (1 Pet. 5:7 NLT) You can pray when you have quiet, focused time—and pray as you go about your busy day. Keep a running list of people and things you're praying for, to help you remember. Or write your prayers like letters to God in your journal, to help you to concentrate when you pray. Use the pictures posted on your refrigerator or in your Facebook newsfeed to prompt you to stop and pray—right then and there.

You can pray that God will move in specific ways or that He will bring about specific outcomes, as you feel led by the Holy Spirit. Or you can pray as Mary did in John 2:3: just tell Jesus the problem, without making any suggestions about what He should do to fix it.[3] (That's actually a lot harder than it sounds.) Pray the Scriptures over yourself and your loved ones. For instance, "I pray that you would strengthen Emily with power through your Spirit in her inner being. . . ." (See Eph. 3:16–19.) Pray the Lord's Prayer, Psalm 23, or some of the beautiful traditional prayers written by great men and women of the faith through the centuries.

Lately, I've been using my cell phone alerts as a "call to prayer." I set the alerts to go off every hour, and when they do, I stop whatever I'm doing for a few seconds to pray. Sometimes I choose a specific prayer focus for the day; other times, I just pray for whoever is in front of me or whatever comes to mind at the time. When I do it for a few days in a row, I find myself watching the clock—anticipating the time, thinking of things to pray for, and praying even when it isn't "time." That's why I do it, really. To get in the habit of prayer. So it becomes a part of me.

When I have a mental block or face an emotional
curveball, a physical challenge, or a spiritual attack, I take
*time to push **pause** and pray. I read the Word and I pray.*
I pray before I panic. I pray before I press forward.
I pray before I pursue my own agenda.

—Pam Farrel

Remember (to a healthy extent) to control the things you can (in a healthy way). By this, I mean do the things you can to make more space in your life—more room to breathe, more room for peace. If clutter really bothers you—if it adds to your stress—then it's worth spending some time getting organized and getting rid of the mess. Are there things you could be doing to accomplish what you need to accomplish more quickly and easily, with less stress? Could you delegate more? Or defer some things to another time, another season? Go through your schedule and take a hard look at your commitments and obligations and responsibilities and see how they line up with your priorities. (We talked about this in Chapter Four.) This time, think in terms of "What is robbing me of my peace?"

Is there any way to change the situation? Get rid of it? Limit your exposure to it? Turn down the noise? If you can't do any of those things, can you change the way you look at it? Change the way you respond to it? Change what you expect from it—or what you expect from yourself? It might be a good idea to talk it over with people you trust and get their perspective.

Remember to take care of your body. You know the stress of trying to run the world can take its toll. Seriously, I don't have to tell you that one of the best things you can do to relieve the physical tension—the aches and pains and the buildup of adrenaline—is to exercise, eat right, and get plenty of fresh air and sunshine. Unfortunately, taking care of our bodies is the first thing (after our quiet time) that we're likely to skip when we feel overwhelmed and exhausted. But that's when we need it (and, coincidentally, our quiet time) the most.

Another reason to take care of our health? Being physically unwell can actually cause symptoms we mistake as the effects of "stress" or other emotional or spiritual indicators. Agitation, anxiety, restlessness, forgetfulness, irritability, lethargy, mood swings . . . these and other symptoms can actually be caused by food sensitivities, medical conditions, or by side effects of certain medications (including over-the-counter supplements and herbal remedies). It may or may not be all the stress you've been under lately. So keep your doctor's appointments and keep on top of your health. Do what you need to do to take care of the body God's given you.

Trust the past to God's mercy, the present to God's love,
and the future to God's providence.
—Saint Augustine

Remember to look for peaceful moments in the middle of your life. And make the most of them, wherever and whenever you find them. You can even learn to create them. But don't live waiting for or working toward that day when everything is perfect, everything is peaceful—in every area of your life. For most of us, that day never comes. Some of us do experience quieter seasons—seasons of rest. We may be able to take a sabbatical from time to time or enjoy our retirement. (If that's the season you find yourself in today, I'd like to encourage you—once in a while—to find a weary, worn-out woman and do something to give her a break!)

But until then, in the meantime, and in case that season never comes, embrace the peaceful moments—those little glimpses of Heaven—that you find along the way. Maybe it's the songbirds in your garden, the beautiful sunset. The first cup of coffee early in the morning, when no one else in the house is awake. The moment before the curtain rises at the concert. Curling up with a good book. Going for a walk on the beach. Rocking your baby or grandbaby (or the babies in the church nursery) to sleep. Savor the peaceful moments, each and every one, as you thank God, and breathe deeply.

The psalmist said, "The LORD is my shepherd; I shall not want. He makes me lie down in green pastures. He leads me beside still waters. He restores my soul" (Ps. 23:1–3 ESV). When we follow the Shepherd, we stop striving, stop struggling, stop fighting, stop trying so hard—to control everyone and everything. To fix everyone and everything. Including ourselves.

We find rest.

We find peace. His peace. Peace that passes (or transcends) all understanding (Phil. 4:7). Peace that isn't dependent on our circumstances. Peace that can weather any storm. And then—this is what's so amazing—we actually become His instruments of peace. He uses us to do what we've wanted to do, what we've been trying to do all along: bring peace into the lives of the people we love and into the world around us.

We get to be His vessels—filled with His peace. His hands, His feet.

It's the paradox so beautifully expressed in the Prayer of St. Francis of Assisi:

Lord, make me an instrument of Your peace.
Where there is hatred, let me sow love; where there
    is injury, pardon;
where there is doubt, faith; where there is despair,
    hope;
where there is darkness, light; where there is
    sadness, joy.

O, Divine Master, grant that I may not so much seek
    to be consoled as to console;
to be understood as to understand; to be loved as
    to love;
For it is in giving that we receive; it is in pardoning
    that we are pardoned;
it is in dying that we are born again to eternal life.

Amen.

Bible Study

1. What does the word "peace" mean to you? What scenes or images come to mind? When have you felt the most peaceful? What brings you peace now? How do you experience moments of peace in your daily life?

Have you ever experienced peace at a time in your life that was anything but peaceful? How? What was that like?

2. Look up Luke 8:22–25 (see also Mark 4:36–41). Why did the disciples find themselves in the middle of a storm? Whose idea was it to sail across the lake?

Where was Jesus?

What did He do? What did the disciples learn about storms? About themselves? About Jesus?

3. Now turn to Acts 12:1–17. What was happening to the disciples? (vv. 1–4)

Who was asleep this time? (v. 7)

How was this possible, given the circumstances? (See Romans 14:8.)

How their faith had grown—and would continue to grow! What did God do? (v. 11)

4. What are the biggest threats to your peace right now? Are you in the middle of some storms—some trials, some major crises? Or are your challenges more the everyday frustrations, the hassles, the constant (minor) conflicts, and steady stream of interruptions?

What are some specific things you can do today—this week—to actively hold on to your peace?

5. Choose one of the following verses—or one mentioned previously in the chapter—to memorize and meditate on this week:

Psalm 29:11	Isaiah 26:3
John 14:27	Romans 15:13
Psalm 119:165	Philippians 4:6–8
John 16:33	2 Thessalonians 3:16

6. Take a few moments to record any further thoughts or reflections in your journal.

Chapter Nine

Letting Go of Worry, Negativity, and Misery

I used to think that it was God's will for us to be holy, not necessarily happy. But I don't believe that anymore. God surely calls us to be holy but He also made us to be happy. Holiness and happiness are not opposites but part of a whole. Holiness leads to wholeness and wholeness leads to happiness.

—Leslie Vernick

As I sat down to write this book, I started by thinking about the biggest challenges that we as women face. I made a list of things that hold us back, weigh us down, or keep us stuck. You know, the things we need to let go, if we want to be free to be the women we were meant to be. As I was brainstorming, I realized that several of them fall under the broad category of attitude, or overall perspective on life.

The first group that came to mind were anxious thoughts, nagging worries, and crippling fears. (I'd just finished writing a book on facing fear.) When we spend all of our time imagining what could go wrong, worrying about what might happen, wondering what we're going to do, and planning how we're going to fix everyone or everything—well, we're pretty miserable. Living with all that pressure and stress, it's hard to be free.

And then there's a negativity that can sometimes get hold of us. A grumbling and complaining "woe is me" mentality.

The world has created a bumper sticker philosophy that reads: "Life is hard and then you die." As Christians, we've adapted it: "Life is hard (but suffering is good for you—it makes you holy!) and then you die (and go to heaven)." It reminds me of six-year-old Calvin, one of my favorite comic book characters, mimicking his dad: "Calvin! Go do something you hate! Being miserable builds character!"[1]

So what if we're miserable now? That's okay, as long as it's building character, as long as it's making us holy—right? But holiness is becoming more and more like Jesus—who had absolute confidence in the will of God for Him and for us. He joyfully and completely trusted His Abba Father, and told us to trust Him, too!

When you are convinced of the character of God, the goodness of God, the power of God, and the love of God— specifically His love for you!—you experience His joy. Nehemiah 8:10 says the joy of the Lord is our strength. That joy is how we face the trials and tribulations of this world. Missionary to China J. Hudson Taylor saw in Jesus three kinds of joy: "His joy in ransoming us, His joy in dwelling within us as our Savior and power for fruit-bearing, and His joy in possessing us as His Bride and delight; it is the consciousness of this joy which is our real strength. Our joy in Him may be a fluctuating thing: His joy in us knows no change."[2]

So knowing how joyful Jesus feels about us—no matter how we feel about Him—gives us courage, confidence, and strength.

Jesus promised his disciples three things—
that they would be completely fearless,
absurdly happy, and in constant trouble.

—G. K. Chesterton

Part of our problem—one reason we sometimes have a hard time being joyful—is that we let our circumstances (or our perspective on our circumstances) dictate our feelings. I recently ran across a story that illustrates the power of perspective—and how it really only comes with time.

> A poor Chinese farmer's only horse runs away. When his neighbor hears this troubling news he says to the farmer, "What bad news! I am so sorry."
>
> The farmer only looks at his neighbor and says, "How do I know this is bad?"
>
> A few days later the horse returns, bringing a wild stallion along. When the neighbor hears about this he says to the farmer, "That's wonderful. What good news."
>
> The farmer looks at him and asks, "How do I know this is good?"
>
> The farmer's only son tries to tame the wild horse and accidentally breaks his leg. Upon hearing of the accident, the neighbor says to the farmer, "What a tragedy this is."
>
> To which the farmer only says, "How do I know this is bad?"
>
> Shortly after that a war breaks out and the emperor requires all young and able-bodied men to fight, but the farmer's only son is spared.[3]

We're so quick to jump to conclusions—perfectly logical, perfectly rational or reasonable, perfectly understandable conclusions. Still, we don't have all the facts. We don't see the big picture. Only God does.

So many times, the things we think of as trials or tribulations or even curses are actually blessings in disguise. It's true with the big things and the small things—the ordinary, everyday frustrations of life. My friend, author and speaker Carole Lewis, says, "Our perspective about what we're going through at any given moment is paramount to the person we ultimately become."[4]

She explains:

Sometimes it seems like there are more bad moments than good in life. The problem is that if we don't stop and take a clear look at our perceptions of these situations, pretty soon we find that we have bitter, negative experiences all day long. Soon enough, having negative experiences all day long turns into having negative experiences every day, every year, every decade. One morning we wake up and discover that these experiences have transformed us. It isn't the situations that are negative now—it's us. We've become bitter, negative people. And we hate who we've become.[5]

The greater part of our happiness or misery
depends on our dispositions, not our circumstances.
We carry the seeds of the one or the other
about with us in our minds wherever we go.

—Martha Washington

Carole is determined not to let that happen to her. In fact, she's one of the most positive, most upbeat, most joyful women I've ever met. It's a delight to spend time with her. Just five minutes and you come away energized, motivated, encouraged, and inspired.

It's all the more amazing when you know her story. For the first twenty or thirty years of their married life, Carole and Johnny faced the same kinds of challenges most people do—running a business, raising a family. They went through some tough times financially and eventually lost their business to bankruptcy. It was hard. It was humbling. But they learned a lot and they lived through it.

Then, in 2001, their thirty-nine-year-old daughter Shari (wife and mother of three teenage girls) was killed by a drunk driver as she stood in the driveway of her in-laws' home on Thanksgiving Day. In 2007, Hurricane Ike completely destroyed their home and swept everything they owned into Galveston Bay. Back in 1997, before they lost Shari and before they lost their home, Johnny had been diagnosed with end-stage cancer that had spread throughout his body. He'd been given less than two years to live. As I write this, it's been seventeen years. With the cancer alone, it's been a seventeen-year roller coaster of chemo and radiation and medication, surgeries, and procedures. There've been relapses and setbacks and miraculous recoveries, followed by more relapses and setbacks and miraculous recoveries. They've spent seventeen years being grateful for each and every day, receiving it as a gift—but never knowing what the next doctor's appointment or blood test or bone scan might reveal. Which Christmas or birthday or anniversary might be the last. And in the meantime, they have grieved the loss of their precious daughter, tried to help their son-in-law raise their granddaughters, and rebuilt their home.

If anyone has a reason to be in a constant state of anxiety, worry, fear, or stress, it's Carole. If anyone has a reason to be miserable, to be bitter or angry or unhappy . . . it's Carole.

But Carole has still found reasons to rejoice, because she is absolutely convinced—as am I (and, I hope, as are you!)—that God is good and that He is sovereign—that He is in control of everything that happens to us. That nothing escapes His notice or His care. Whatever comes our way has to first come through His hands. And He is able to work all things—*all things*—together for our good (Rom. 8:28).*

Listen to what He says:

> Fear not, for I have redeemed you; I have called you by name, you are mine. (Isa. 43:1 ESV)

> "For I know the plans I have for you," declares the LORD, "plans to prosper you and not to harm you, plans to give you hope and a future." (Jer. 29:11)

> "Never will I leave you; never will I forsake you." (Heb. 13:5)

Whatever comes our way, we know that there's a purpose—it's not pointless or meaningless, not an accident or an "oops." And

---

*Not long after I wrote this chapter, the day after their fifty-fifth wedding anniversary, Johnny went home to be with the Lord. Carole shared recently with friends and family, "I am doing well and trusting Jesus to be all He promised us He would be. He is sufficient and I love Him more and more every day."

there's a plan—a way out or a way through. And there's an opportunity—to gain something, to give something, to grow something, and always—*always*—a way to bring glory to Him.

How do we do that? "Rejoice always, pray continually, give thanks in all circumstances; for this is God's will for you in Christ Jesus" (1 Thess. 5:16–18 NIV 2011).

All our difficulties are only platforms for the manifestations of His grace, power, and love.

—Hudson Taylor

Holding on to worry, negativity, and misery only makes life harder than it is—harder than it has to be. It makes mountains out of molehills. It makes actual mountains into monstrosities. And it causes us to miss the best of what life can be.

All too often we let worry, negativity, and misery rob us of our ability to be the women God created us to be—rob us of the ability to experience Him and the life He's given us fully. Keep us from taking on the challenges, the adventures, the opportunities that would be so meaningful, so rewarding and fulfilling.

Jesus is calling to us, but sometimes we're so full of doubt and fear that we won't even look over the edge of the boat, let alone step out of it! Remember the scene in Matthew 14:22–33, where Jesus came walking out to meet His disciples on the sea? At first they were terrified. They thought they were seeing a ghost!

But Jesus says, "Take courage! It is I."

That's how we translate it into proper English, anyway. But if you look at the text notes in your Bible, you'll see that what He actually said was, "Take courage! I AM." As in, "I AM THAT I AM." That's the name God gave Moses at the burning bush. The Eternal, the Everlasting, the One who was and who is and who is to come. (See Ex. 3:18, Deut. 33:27, and Rev. 1:8.)

When you realize that's Who you're talking to—that's Who you call your friend (or Who calls you His friend)—how can you be afraid of anything ever again?

Peter replies, "Lord, if it's really you, tell me to come to you." Jesus says simply, "Come!"

I once heard a pastor who was preaching on this passage point out that Jesus always supplies all the power, the ability, the grace, and the strength we need to accomplish whatever it is that He asks us to do. It's inherent in the command. So when He asks us to do something, we don't have to wonder *if* we will be able to do it. We know that we can. Even if that means walking on water.

Mulling it over, I found myself picturing my five-year-old nephew Timmy—love of my life, apple of my eye! We love to do craft projects together. I used to be a teacher, so you can believe me when I say that Timmy is exceptionally handsome and amazingly talented and incredibly smart. He has a fabulous personality!

With one funny little quirk. Every time he's faced with a new challenge or opportunity, Timmy responds with these two words: "I can't."

It's so silly. He loves to learn. He loves to play. He loves to create. But before I even hand him the scissors or glue or paint, he declares he can't do whatever I'm about to ask him to do. He hasn't even tried. Most of the time he doesn't even know what it is. Doesn't matter.

"I can't."

It's like an automatic reflex.

I'm not really sure what's at the root of it. It could be a lack of confidence. Insecurity. Fear of failure. (Boy, it starts early, doesn't it?) He may have inherited some of Auntie's perfectionism: "If I don't think I can do it perfectly the first time, I don't want to try." Or some of Daddy's . . . um . . . overall outlook on life. (There's a reason we used to call my brother Eeyore.) Sometimes it's laziness. "That looks like work! I don't feel like making the effort. . . ."

But, regardless, my response is always the same: "Yes, you can . . . see!"

Because there are three things to know about every project I put in front of Timmy:

- **I chose it specifically for him.** I prepared it ahead of time. I had a plan and a purpose in mind. I knew before I brought it to him that he was fully capable of accomplishing the task, *or* (being a teacher) I knew that he needed to learn the skill involved and that this is the way to learn it.
- **I have already equipped him**. I've prepared him through other projects we've worked on together. And I've provided him with all of the supplies and tools he needs. Because I want him to succeed.

- **I'm not going anywhere.** I will be right there beside him, ready to help—every step of the way.

Most of the time, after one or two I can'ts, Timmy joyfully discovers that he can—and we make memories, as well as messy craft projects together! But, occasionally, the I can'ts persist. Stubborn and whiny or whimpering. It may be fear or insecurity at the root of it . . . it may be laziness or even disobedience.

That's when I smile and say—lovingly, sweetly, firmly—in my best teacher voice:

"You *can* . . . and you *will*!"

And he does.

To bring it back to Peter and the boat, maybe Jesus has called you, as He's called me, to step out in certain areas of our lives. Step out in obedience and faith. Frankly, some of the things He's calling me to do scare me! I find myself suddenly filled with fear, anxiety, insecurity, or doubt. Other things look like too much effort, too much work.

I start to lift my foot. I might even get over the side of the boat. But then I turn back.

"I can't . . . I can't do this . . . really . . . I can't."

But Jesus is reminding me that every task He's called me to is one He's chosen and prepared especially. He knows that I'm able—or need to be able. He's equipped me with everything I need. And He's right there with me, ready to help me every step of the way.

Just like I am with Timmy.

On those days—when I feel myself shrinking back, when I hear myself saying "I can't"—it's as if Jesus is gently tipping my chin up, making me look Him right in the eye, as He answers lovingly, firmly:

"Yes, you *can*. And you *will!*"

He's right, of course.

I have to let go of my worries, my doubts, my insecurities, and my fears. Let go of my negativity.

I can. And I will.

And I do.

Because I don't ever want to miss out on the opportunity, the experience, the adventure, the blessing—the time spent with Him—because of a bad attitude.

Bible Study

1. If you were to give yourself a report card on your attitude, overall you'd have to score it . . .

☐ Excellent   ☐ Good
☐ Satisfactory   ☐ Needs Improvement

Which areas do you struggle with the most?

☐ Worry/Anxiety/Fear
☐ Grumbling/Complaining
☐ Expecting/Believing the Worst

How might it be hurting you or holding you back?

2. Sometimes it helps to remember how far we've come—some of the amazing, "impossible" things God has already done in us and through us. What's something that you've accomplished—by God's grace—that you never thought you could do?

3. Look up each of the following Scriptures and record what you learn from each one about God's will—His desire—for us:

   a) 2 Timothy 1:7

   b) Philippians 4:4–7

   c) Philippians 2:14–15

   d) Philippians 4:12–13

   e) Philippians 4:8

4. Choose one of the following verses—or one mentioned previously in the chapter—to memorize and meditate on this week.

Psalm 23	Matthew 6:34
Hebrews 11:1	Luke 18:27
1 Peter 5:7	Matthew 6:33
Hebrews 11:6	Matthew 17:20

5. Take a few moments to record any further thoughts or reflections in your journal.

Chapter Ten

Holding On to Joy

To be surprised by joy is the most wonderful thing,
to be reminded that your heart is pumping blood
around your body and your eyes are awake to what's
going on in the world and what's happening to you,
and to give thanks.

—Bono

When I was a young girl, I read a lot of stories of courageous women who triumphed over adversity, extraordinary women whose faith was forged in the crucible of pain and suffering. There was something so beautiful about it, so noble. Although I couldn't have articulated it then, I understood that these women had a strength of character and a spiritual depth I longed for. Though I knew it was foolish to even think such a thing—sometimes I secretly wished that something terrible would happen to me (like being paralyzed or losing my sight) so that I could be one of those kinds of women.

Imagine my surprise when—long after I had outgrown that phase—I experienced my share of pain and suffering (more than my share, it seemed), including some health issues that confined me to bed for months at a time and left me with chronic pain—and guess what? It didn't feel very noble at all.

It didn't make me deep and spiritual. It made me cranky. Really cranky. Irritable. Frustrated. Aggravated. Impatient. I got to see sides to my personality I didn't know were there. Whiny sides, mostly. Grumbling sides, complaining sides. Selfish sides. Stubborn sides.

Instead of being filled with faith, I fell headlong into discouragement and despair. At times, I felt like every new hurt or hardship was just further evidence that God didn't really love me, that He had rejected me or abandoned me. I was hurt. I was angry.

My parents thought I threw impressive tantrums when I was two. They were nothing compared to the ones Jesus has seen since. It took awhile for me to work through all of that. But Jesus is patient, as well as gentle and kind. I know now that He loves me. I am absolutely convinced of that. I believe in the deepest part of my being that He has chosen me and not rejected me (Isa. 41:9). That He will never leave me nor forsake me (Heb. 13:5; Matt. 28:20). I know I can trust Him and His sovereignty—rest in His will for me. I can be still (Ps. 46:10).

But lately I've found that "being still" isn't enough for me. I mean, I'm glad I'm not throwing tantrums anymore. But I've discovered that—sometimes—all it really means is that I'm suffering in silence. Stuffing all the hurt and frustration and disappointment and trying to ignore it. Pretending it isn't there or that it doesn't matter.

I've accidentally adopted a kind of "suck it up and deal with it" mentality, a spiritual stoicism. A resignation that is miles away from acceptance with joy. The crankiness is what gives me a clue. The scowl I feel my face settling into. The overall crabbiness or moodiness. It tells me my heart still has work to do.

I keep coming back to this little poem from the classic devotional *Streams in the Desert*. It speaks to the difference between stoicism and being still, between being still on the surface and truly settling your heart in Him.

I will be still, my bruised heart faintly murmured,
As o'er me rolled a crushing load of woe;
The cry, the call, e'en the low moan was stifled;
I pressed my lips; I barred the tear drop's flow.

I will be still, although I cannot see it,
The love that bares a soul and fans pain's fire;
That takes away the last sweet drop of solace,
Breaks the lone harp string, hides Thy precious lyre.

But God is love, so I will bide me, bide me—
We'll doubt not, Soul, we will be very still;
We'll wait till after while, when He shall lift us
Yes, after while, when it shall be His will.

And I did listen to my heart's brave promise;
And I did quiver, struggling to be still;
And I did lift my tearless eyes to Heaven,
Repeating ever, "Yea, Christ, have Thy will."

But soon my heart upspake from 'neath our burden,
Reproved my tight-drawn lips, my visage sad:
"We can do more than this, O Soul," it whispered.
"We can be more than still, we can be glad!"[1]

Joy does not simply happen to us.
We have to choose joy and keep choosing it every day.

—Henri Nouwen

See, it's one thing to let go of worry, negativity, and misery. To stop whining, stop grumbling, stop complaining. To choose to stop having a bad attitude. It's another thing to cheerfully embrace the will of God for us—whatever it is—in absolute trust, absolute faith, absolute confidence in our loving Heavenly Father. To actively choose to have a *good* attitude. To choose *joy*.

That's what I want—what I believe Jesus wants for me. And for you.

There are times when it's a lot easier than others. And it seems to come easier to some people than others. But with a little practice, with a little effort, with a little determination, it's something every one of us can do. Before you know it, it'll become a part of you.

Did you know that laughter or cheerfulness is one of the attributes of the idealized Proverbs 31 woman? Proverbs 31:25 says she laughs at the days to come—she's not worried or afraid; she's cheerful and confident about the future. Because she knows who holds the future. She's done all she can do. Her times are in His hands (Ps. 31:15).

The psalmist said over and over that with His love for us, with all the wonderful things He has done for us, God has filled us with joy and laughter, and that He has made us glad. We've just got to hold on to it!

My best friend has a cartoon on her refrigerator of two elderly women, one of them with a dazed-looking devil fallen at her feet. Clearly, she's just smacked him over the head with her oversized purse. She's explaining to her friend, "He tried to steal my joy!" I think all I'm trying to say in this chapter is: Ladies, we aren't having none of that!

Following are some great ways to hold on tight to the joy of the Lord.

Don't let your spirit get "hangry." Have you heard that word? It's a combination of hungry and angry. If you google it, you'll see it's defined (humorously) as "a state of anger caused by a lack of food; strong feelings of annoyance, displeasure or hostility aroused by hunger." Hunger from dieting, usually, or from accidentally skipping a meal or two. It's true: when your body is starving, that low blood sugar can make you feel tired and cranky and sometimes trigger an emotional outburst. And the same is true when your spirit is starving—when it hasn't been fed.

We feed our spirits by spending time with Jesus. In His presence is "fullness of joy" (Ps. 16:11 ESV). I love how Emily Freeman describes it:

> God's Spirit indwells us in the same way we are to let His Word dwell richly within us. It is not only remaining in Christ; it is letting Christ remain in you. It is not only memorizing Scripture and having a Bible study; it is letting the person of Jesus Christ take up residence within you, not as a timid house-guest, but as the abundant provider, the bread-winner, the respected head of the household, the host. He doesn't sit at your table, feeble and frail, waiting for you to feed Him by reading your Bible and praying. He stands strong at the head, graciously filling your plate with all that He is. He lavishes us with

a godly inheritance. The riches of the fruit of His
Spirit are made available to us in abundant supply.[2]

The fruit of His Spirit—including joy! Practically speaking,
there are a hundred and one ways to connect with Him and
be fed by Him throughout your day. Yes, those include focused
one-on-one time with Him, your quiet time or devotions. But
also consider the time you spend talking to Him while you
weed your garden or do the dishes or walk a few laps around
the neighborhood. The time you spend in church and in small
group Bible studies or in informal get-togethers with friends
who pray with you and encourage you in the Lord. The time
you spend on behalf of the ministries you participate in—at the
food pantry, with the choir or youth. The praise and worship
and the preaching and teaching that you listen to on your MP3
player or in the car. The books and magazines you read. The
Scriptures you have posted around the house. The inspirational
e-mails and Facebook posts and videos. The gratitude journal
you fill in before you fall asleep at night. It all counts. It all
helps. It all feeds your spirit and helps you hold on to your joy!

Guard your heart and mind. It's one thing to be aware of
what's going on in the world around you—to know that there
are people in desperate need, to have your heart broken for
them, and to be motivated to do something to help them, for
Jesus' sake. (See the next suggestion.) It's another thing to allow
yourself to be filled with worry or fear or stress, hopelessness
or depression, envy or jealousy or competition, anger or hate or
hostility or aggression—because of the things you read online
or see on TV or hear from your friends. Now, more than ever,

there are so many voices screaming for your attention, insisting that you must listen to them or else. . . .

But Proverbs 4:23 warns us, "Above all else, guard your heart, for it is the wellspring of life." The New Living Translation says, "Guard your heart above all else, for it determines the course of your life." If you're going to hold on to your joy, you're going to have to set some boundaries, some limits. There are things you're going to have to choose not to watch, not to read, not to listen to. Maybe even some people you choose not to spend too much time with. Your boundaries may be different from mine. And they may be different for you at different times in your life. You use the discernment God has given you to determine what's best for you.

Replace the negative influences with positive ones. Look for books, movies, magazines, cartoons, and clever sayings that are funny or inspirational or uplifting. Listen to happy music (any kind). Find things that make you smile, make you laugh—and keep them all around you. Life is hard, but it doesn't have to be miserable. You don't *lose* points for finding joy in the journey, as you "suffer for Jesus." You gain!

> *It is pleasing to God whenever thou rejoicest or laughest from the bottom of thy heart.*
>
> —Martin Luther

Lighten someone else's load. Believe it or not, one of the best ways to hold on to your joy is to share it with someone else. Look for someone who needs joy, someone who needs love, needs laughter, needs encouragement or motivation or inspiration—and give it to them! Look for someone who's hurting, someone who's struggling or suffering. And help them. Comfort them. Serve them.

Send them a little gift, a note, an e-mail, or a text. Take them to lunch or a movie; go for a walk or cruise garage sales. Give them a ride to the doctor or dentist. Make them a meal or do a few loads of laundry for them; help them with a household project that's gotten out of hand. Whatever it is they need . . . ask them, but make some suggestions, so they know the kinds of things you're willing or able to do. Be the hands and feet of Jesus and, as you do, His joy will flow through you.

Keep your eyes on the prize (Phil. 3:14). Remember who you are. Remember Who and what you're living for. So much of what frustrates and irritates and upsets us, so much of what worries and stresses us, so much of what threatens to steal our joy—it's so minor, so petty, so inconsequential, so small, so temporary in the light of eternity. In light of what really and truly matters.

Even the things that seem so huge, so impossible, so overwhelming pale in comparison.

Here's the truth, according to the Apostle Paul:

We are hard pressed on every side, but not crushed; perplexed, but not in despair; persecuted, but not abandoned; struck down, but not destroyed. . . .

Therefore we do not lose heart. Though outwardly we are wasting away, yet inwardly we are being renewed day by day. For our light and momentary troubles are achieving for us an eternal glory that far outweighs them all. So we fix our eyes not on what is seen, but on what is unseen. For what is seen is temporary, but what is unseen is eternal. (2 Cor. 4:8–9, 16–18)

―――――――――――――――――――――――――

There are two ways of getting out of a trial. One is to simply try to get rid of the trial, and be thankful when it is over. The other is to recognize the trial as a challenge from God to claim a larger blessing than we have ever had, and to hail it with delight as an opportunity of obtaining a larger measure of divine grace.

—A. B. Simpson

―――――――――――――――――――――――――

Years ago, my dad first told me a version of this story.

Two young girls—sisters—were ecstatic to hear they'd be spending the summer with their grandparents on the family farm, way out in the country. All that fresh air and sunshine and fun! Grandma had promised that they could help her plant her garden and that she'd teach them how to bake her world-famous flaky biscuits. After some cajoling, Grandpa promised they could help him with the animals—just like real farmhands!

But the day he let them come to work with him wasn't quite what they expected. Maintaining a farm and taking care of animals is hard work! It was still early in the morning when they found themselves standing in the barn, facing a mountain of . . . well . . . poop. Grandpa handed them shovels and told them where it all needed to go. Just then, he was called away to another part of the farm—some kind of emergency with one of the cows.

The first sister stared at the great, stinking heap and burst into tears. She had wanted to be a real farmhand—but not if it meant this!

"It's not fair . . . this is too hard . . . I don't want to do this!" she cried, as she ran back to the house and into Grandma's arms.

Four hours later, Grandpa returned to the barn—where he was astonished to find the second sister working away at the mountain of manure. She was filthy and her little hands were covered in blisters. But she had a smile on her face—she was even humming a cheerful little song.

When he asked her why she was still there, still working so hard—why she hadn't gotten bored or given up or thrown a tantrum like her sister and run away—she said: "Well, with all this poop, there's gotta be a pony in here somewhere!"

I don't know about you, but I've been facing a lot of poop lately. Stuff at home, stuff at work, stuff at church. Financial stuff, health stuff. Friends-and-family stuff. Big stuff and little stuff. Some of it just aggravating or frustrating, some of it disappointing, even heartbreaking.

It would be easy to lose perspective. I could throw a tantrum or let loose a torrent of tears. Or I could sit in the corner silently, shaking from the effort of keeping it all in. Been there, done that. Didn't like where it got me. Or more accurately, where it *didn't* get me.

So instead I've decided I'm keeping my eyes open for the pony! That's how I'm holding on to my joy. I'm looking for the gifts, the blessings, the opportunities in the midst of it all—the gifts, blessings, and opportunities God promises are really there. Things to learn and grow from. Things to celebrate. Things to be thankful for. Things that point me to and keep me dependent on Him. I keep a list of these things in my journal—which is full to overflowing.

And I keep a little purple pony on my desk, to remind me not to let the poop get the better of me. Whatever comes my way today, I'm going to face cheerfully—joyfully—with shovel in hand, ready to get to work. Because I know there's a pony in there somewhere. And I'm telling you right now, that pony is mine!

Bible Study

1. Can you think of some "ponies"—unexpected blessings in the midst of trials and tribulations—that God has brought to you? What good things have come out of the tough times you've faced?

2. Look up each of the Scriptures and answer the questions below:
   a) According to Hebrews 12:2, why did Jesus endure the suffering He experienced on the cross?

   b) In Luke 10:21, the disciples had just come back from their first missions trip, and they were excited about all the amazing things they had learned. How did Jesus feel?

c) In John 15:11, what did Jesus say He wanted us to experience?

d) In John 10:10, why (or for what purpose) did Jesus say He had come?

Different translations use the words "abundantly," or "in all its fullness," or "that they may enjoy it to the full, til it overflows."

3. For the most part, does this—John 10:10—describe your life today? If not, why not? What would need to change? What's within your power to change?

4. Choose one of the following verses—or one mentioned previously in the chapter—to memorize and meditate on this week.

Psalm 16:11	James 1:2
1 Thessalonians 5:16–18	Colossians 3:16
Psalm 28:7	James 1:12
Ephesians 5:19b–20	1 Peter 5:10

5. Take a few moments to record any further thoughts or reflections in your journal.

Chapter Eleven

Letting Go of Lesser Things

*When I see the elaborate study and ingenuity
displayed by women in the pursuit of trifles,
I feel no doubt of their capacity for the most
Herculean undertakings.*

—Julia Ward Howe

*T*he title of this chapter comes from a hymn written in the early 1900s. I've adapted the words just a little. Well, one word:

> Rise up, O *women* of God!
> Have done with lesser things.
> Give heart and mind and soul and strength
> To serve the King of kings.[1]

The verses that follow talk about how the days grow long and dark and Jesus has yet to return (though it must be soon), and there are still so many battles to be fought and won! So much kingdom work to be done. Not like dull, meaningless chores. More things to add to our endless to-dos.

Important, exciting, meaningful, fulfilling, eternally significant things!

So it's time we let go of lesser things—"everything that hinders and the sin that so easily entangles" so that we can "run with perseverance the race marked out for us" (Heb. 12:1). Lesser things compete with Jesus for our love and devotion. They distract us or deter us from answering His call. They sidetrack us, they stall us. If we let them, they will keep us from accomplishing His purposes for us. Even good things can become bad, if they keep us from the best.

If you've made it this far into the book, you know that by "lesser things" I can't possibly mean simple pleasures—the many precious gifts God has given us to enjoy. Just because we enjoy something does not in any way make it "lesser." Nor does the fact that we may or may not be able to ascribe to it any useful purpose or meaning or eternal significance. God went out of His way to make the world beautiful because He could. Because He wanted to. Because it's who He is. He meant for us to appreciate it and enjoy it. And to appreciate and enjoy the creativity He's put in us and the people around us.

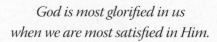

God is most glorified in us
when we are most satisfied in Him.
—John Piper

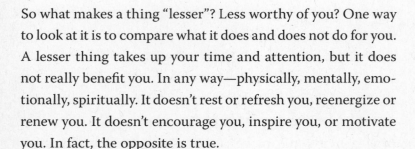

So what makes a thing "lesser"? Less worthy of you? One way to look at it is to compare what it does and does not do for you. A lesser thing takes up your time and attention, but it does not really benefit you. In any way—physically, mentally, emotionally, spiritually. It doesn't rest or refresh you, reenergize or renew you. It doesn't encourage you, inspire you, or motivate you. In fact, the opposite is true.

A lesser thing usually demotivates you. It seems to dull your appetite for better things, more meaningful things, particularly spiritual things. Ultimately it becomes unrewarding, unful-filling, unproductive.

At its worst, it can be addictive. It can lead you to make irresponsible choices, to neglect other, more important things. Or people. Which makes you feel guilty and irritable and defensive. Maybe—for whatever reason—it ends up leading to unhealthy fantasy or it stirs up pride or envy or jealousy, or a critical, judgmental spirit. Maybe you find yourself using it to self-medicate—to escape or numb emotional pain. Maybe you turn to it to feed an emotional or spiritual need, a need that only God can fill (that's actually the biblical definition of idolatry).

So the thing itself may not be a sin. It may not lead others to sin. But it leads you to sin. So for you, it is a sin. "Dear friends, I urge you . . . to abstain from sinful desires, which wage war against your soul" (1 Pet. 2:11). We all struggle with sin and temptation. Most of us have specific areas—specific battlegrounds—where those struggles take place. We have our own specific weaknesses.

"Temptation comes from our own desires, which entice us and drag us away. These desires give birth to sinful actions. And when sin is allowed to grow, it gives birth to death" (James 1:14–15 NLT). If we continually choose not to fight—if we just give in or give up—we will continually be weighed down by guilt, shame, and regret. We can spend all of our time trying to let go of the guilt, or we can spend at least some of the time figuring out how *not* to give in to the sin in the first place. Maybe it's time.

"God blesses those who patiently endure testing and temptation. Afterward they will receive the crown of life that God has promised to those who love him" (James 1:12 NLT). Maybe it's time to confront some of these issues, call them what they are, face them head-on. And by God's grace, in His strength, find a way to beat them.

> For the grace of God has appeared that offers salvation to all people. It teaches us to say "No" to ungodliness and worldly passions, and to live self-controlled, upright and godly lives in this present age, while we wait for the blessed hope—the appearing of the glory of our great God and Savior, Jesus Christ, who gave himself for us to redeem us from all wickedness and to purify for himself a people that are his very own, eager to do what is good. (Titus 2:11–14 NIV 2011)

The reason why many fail in battle is because they wait until the hour of battle. The reason why others succeed is that they have gained their victory on their knees long before the battle came. . . . Anticipate your battles; fight them on your knees before temptation comes, and you will always have victory.

—R. A. Torrey

If we don't confront these issues, we may lose far too much of our precious time on lesser things. And miss our true calling.

"I urge you to live a life worthy of the calling you have received" (Eph. 4:1). Over and over the Scriptures remind us that our lives are not meant to be wasted. The years God has given us aren't meant to be empty and meaningless. God created us for a purpose, a reason. Jesus died to save us for a purpose, a reason.

There's the eternal purpose we all share—"to glorify God and enjoy Him forever."[2] Which is an awesome thought. Literally, as in awe-inspiring—all by itself.

But then there's also the unique, individual purpose for which He has created each one of us. As the psalmist exclaimed:

O LORD, you have searched me and you know me.

You know when I sit and when I rise;
you perceive my thoughts from afar.
You discern my going out and my lying down;
you are familiar with all my ways.
Before a word is on my tongue, you know it completely,
O LORD. . . .

For you created my inmost being;
you knit me together in my mother's womb.
I praise you because I am fearfully and
wonderfully made;
Your works are wonderful, I know that full well.

My frame was not hidden from you when I was made
in the secret place.
When I was woven together in the depths of the earth,
your eyes saw my unformed body.

All the days ordained for me were written in your book

before one of them came to be.
(Ps. 139:1–4, 13–16)

Henri Nouwen observes, "We seldom realize fully that we are sent to fulfill God-given tasks. We act as if we were simply dropped down in creation and have to decide to entertain ourselves until we die. But we were sent into the world by God, just as Jesus was. Once we start living our lives with that conviction, we will soon know what we were sent to do."[3]

The Bible tells us we live in a war-torn world. There is a battle raging all around us—a spiritual battle between the armies of God and the forces of darkness. This unseen battle takes place in the "heavenly realms." And whether we realize it or not, we are a part of it. In fact, we're right in the middle of it. But not as helpless spectators or innocent bystanders. Each one of us is a warrior for one side or the other.

As C. S. Lewis observed, "There is no neutral ground in the universe; every square inch, every split second, is claimed by God and counter-claimed by Satan."[4] God has chosen us. "He has rescued us from the dominion of darkness and brought us into the kingdom of the Son He loves, in whom we have redemption, the forgiveness of sins" (Col. 1:13–14).

And now He has called us into this battle, into this fight. Whatever our task, whatever our role, there are at least four things we all need.

First, we need a vision—an understanding of our own calling. We need to seek God for His specific plan and purpose for us—what He has created us to do. And we need to keep seeking Him, especially as we sense that a season in our lives is changing. It's not that His plan for us changes, but that our understanding of it (sometimes) does—as we get to new places in our journey. To put it another way, I've found God often gives us a general sense of our mission, our passion, our cause, or our theme—which is super helpful in determining our overall direction, ruling in a lot of things and ruling out a lot of others. But what it means to live out that mission day to day is something He usually reveals one step at a time. So we look to Him—and keep looking to Him—for His direction, day by day.

Next, we need guidance to know what—if anything—we can do to better inform ourselves or better prepare ourselves for the tasks ahead. Often we find that God Himself has been preparing us, all along. Our background, our personality, our life experiences, our skills and talents, our special interests— they all come together to make us the perfect person for the job!

Then again, God sometimes stretches us by putting us in a position we feel completely unqualified for. It means we have to lean hard on Him. And quickly figure out what things we need to learn, what skills we need to acquire, which gifts we need to develop to better serve our calling—and our Creator.

We also need a willingness to make the sacrifices that are necessary to answer God's call—and clear direction as to what those sacrifices are. How can we make more of our time and energy and resources available to God? As we look at our current commitments and responsibilities and activities, what do we need to hold on to and what are we willing to let go?

*If you read history you will find that the Christians who
did the most for the present world were precisely those
who thought most of the next. It is since Christians have
largely ceased to think of the other world that they have
become so ineffective in this world.*

—C. S. Lewis

One thing we especially need is courage—a holy boldness.
In a song called "Run to the Battle," Christian recording artist
Steve Camp says, "Some people want to live within the sound
of chapel bells, but I want to run a mission a yard from the
gates of hell."[5] Now that's holy boldness.

I have to admit I more often identify with J. R. R. Tolkien's
hobbit hero Frodo in *The Lord of the Rings* movie. Frodo sees
that the lines have been drawn for the ultimate battle of good
and evil. And the good are terribly outnumbered. The growing darkness—the corruption of what was once good and
true—is oppressive. His quest to destroy the evil ring of power
seems hopeless.

"I wish the ring had never come to me," Frodo exclaims.
"I wish none of this had ever happened." His friend Gandalf
replies, "So do all who live to see such times, but that is not
for them to decide. All we have to decide is what to do with
the time that is given to us."[6]

Reading through the letters to the early church in the New
Testament, we can tell that many of those first disciples felt
the same kind of discouragement. Hard-pressed on every side,

under attack from within and without, persecuted, suffering—they struggled to hold on to hope.

But the apostles reminded them of the ultimate victory that was theirs in Christ—and challenged them in the meantime to be courageous, to stand fast, and to fight the good fight (1 Cor. 16:13), "making the most of every opportunity, because the days are evil" (Eph. 5:16).

These words first written to them were also written for you and me.

It's time to be the warrior princess that—as daughter of the King of kings—you were meant to be. Let go of guilt, shame, and regret. Let go of impossible standards and unrealistic expectations. Let go of hurt, bitterness, and unforgiveness. Let go of the illusion of control. Let go of worry, negativity, and misery. Let go of lesser things.

It's time to strap on your sword and go to war.

"Be strong in the Lord and in his mighty power. Put on the full armor of God so that you can take your stand against the devil's schemes" (Eph. 6:10–11). Fight every battle you find yourself in. Fight to win! Rescue as many prisoners of darkness as you can—and if you can't rescue them (if they don't want to be rescued or they aren't your mission, your assignment), still show them what God's mercy looks like (Jude 1:23). And "live holy and godly lives as you look forward to the day of God and speed its coming" (2 Pet. 3:11–12).

Some of us are called day after day to fight our own personal battles against depression, guilt, discouragement, and defeat. Every day that we get out of bed and pick up our sword is another victory. Every day we keep fighting, keep looking forward to the day that Jesus sets us completely, once-and-for-all free.

Many of us do battle on behalf of our families, our friends, our churches, our communities, our nations, or even countries overseas. There are so many important causes, so many desperate needs.

We battle by praying, believing, and encouraging. By loving, giving, and serving. We battle by protecting and defending. We battle by leading and guiding, teaching and mentoring. We battle by setting a good example. By standing up for truth and righteousness. We battle by speaking the truth in love.

Every good, God-honoring choice we make, every act of obedience, every loving sacrifice, every selfless deed, every gift, every kindness, every prayer . . . it makes a difference. It counts. "But thanks be to God, Who in Christ always leads us in triumph [as trophies of Christ's victory] and through us spreads *and* makes evident the fragrance of the knowledge of God everywhere" (2 Cor. 2:14 AMP).

Or, as some translations put it, "the sweet perfume."

What an awesome privilege! What an incredible responsibility!

But it's something we can only do if we're willing to let go of lesser things.

Bible Study

1. Right now, at this time in your life, what has God called you to do? What relationships, what responsibilities, what ministries has He given you? What passions? What gifts or talents? What dreams or desires for the future?

If you really don't know, ask Him to show you. Spend some time over the next few days or weeks thinking about it and praying about it. Talk to the people who are your trusted friends or mentors or encouragers. Ask them what they see.

2. What are the "lesser things" in your life right now—the distractions, the hindrances, the obstacles, maybe the unconquered sins—that keep you from being who God made you to be and doing what God made you to do?

3. What can you do about these things—specifically, concretely? What are some choices you could make, some steps you could take? Where could you find help or accountability, if you needed to? Will you?

4. Look up each of the following verses and jot down what you learn from them about living a holy (God-honoring) life.

Colossians 2:6–7:

Colossians 2:8:

Colossians 3:1–2:

Colossians 3:5–10:

Colossians 3:12–14:

Colossians 3:15:

Colossians 3:16:

Colossians 3:17:

5. Choose one of the verses above—or one mentioned previously in the chapter—to memorize and meditate on this week.

6. Take a few moments to record any further thoughts or reflections in your journal.

Chapter Twelve

Holding On to Hope

When you get into a tight place and everything goes against you, till it seems as though you could not hang on a minute longer, never give up then, for that is just the place and time that the tide will turn.

—**Harriet Beecher Stowe**

There's a powerful scene in the movie version of *The Lord of the Rings: The Two Towers*, where King Théoden of Rohan finds himself in a desperate battle. One he cannot hope to win. His kingdom is under siege. His armies are hopelessly outnumbered. His people will not survive the night.

And it's all his fault. Or, at least, it feels that way. His kingdom began crumbling long ago, when he was distracted. When he fell under the influence of an evil spirit. When he listened to the lies of the enemy and was deceived. When he made a series of poor choices that devastated everyone around him. While he was held captive.

He's free now. Seeing clearly, thinking clearly for the first time in a long time. But it's too late. He can't go back and undo what's been done. He can't rally his people, strengthen them, prepare them for battle in time. They cannot withstand the onslaught of the enemy.

Realizing he has utterly failed his people and himself, Théoden is overcome by guilt and despair, shame and regret. He quotes the haunting words of a poem:

Where is the horse and the rider?
Where is the horn that was blowing?
They have passed like rain on the mountain,
Like wind in the meadow.
The days have gone down in the West,
Behind the hills into shadow.
How did it come to this?[1]

That last line echoed in my own heart a few years ago. I found myself in a very dark place, spiritually, emotionally, and physically. It felt like my life was in shambles. I had been listening to the enemy. Everywhere I looked, I could see only failure and defeat.

I stood in church one morning during the worship service, tears running down my face. Overwhelmed by all my failures and mistakes, the poor choices I'd made. Looking at the future with hopelessness, filled with fear and dread.

That image of King Théoden was stuck in my head, as I whispered in despair: "How did it come to this?"

I could barely keep from sobbing out loud.

But that Sunday morning—as I stood there, absolutely shattered—it was like the Holy Spirit reached into my mind where that image from the movie had been frozen on the screen and hit "play."

I remembered what happens next.

Théoden and his companions are about to ride out one final time, prepared to meet their deaths on the battlefield. Suddenly, they realize it's dawn. The long night is over. A rider on a white horse appears on the top of the hill, with a vast army behind him, come to the rescue. The rider charges down to meet the enemy, with a blinding light that decimates the darkness.

I saw heaven standing open and there before me
was a white horse, whose rider is called Faithful and
True. With justice he judges and wages war. His
eyes are like blazing fire, and on his head are many
crowns. . . . The armies of heaven were following
him. . . . On his robe and on his thigh he has this
name written: KING OF KINGS AND LORD OF LORDS.
(Rev. 19:11–16)

Jesus reminded me that in my darkest moments, I am not
without hope, not without help (2 Cor. 4:9).

He is with me.

And He's bringing with Him victory.

That's what He's put on my heart to remind you today: no
matter how dark it seems in your life or the life of someone
you love, take courage. Press on. Have faith. Hold on to hope.

And keep your eyes on the skies, for the King of Glory, "thy
King cometh unto thee" (Ps. 24:7, Zech. 9:9 KJV).

> *God is the only one who can make*
> *the valley of trouble a door of hope.*
>
> —Catherine Marshall

It's not easy to hold on to hope—even a hope as glorious as
ours. Sometimes it's hard for us to fully grasp what it means.
I love how Paul prays for the Ephesians and for us:

I keep asking that the God of our Lord Jesus Christ,
the glorious Father, may give you the Spirit of wisdom

and revelation, so that you may know him better. I
pray that the eyes of your heart may be enlightened
*in order that you may know the hope to which he has
called you,* the riches of his glorious inheritance in
his holy people, and his incomparably great power for
us who believe. That power is the same as the mighty
strength he exerted when he raised Christ from the
dead and seated him at his right hand in the heavenly
realms, far above all rule and authority, power and
dominion, and every name that is invoked, not only
in the present age but also in the one to come. (Eph.
1:17–21 NIV 2011; emphasis mine)

---

*While Jesus calls each of us to a more perfect life,
we cannot achieve it on our own. To be alive is to be
broken; to be broken is to stand in need of grace. It is only
through grace that any of us could dare to hope
that we could become more like Christ.*

—Brennan Manning

Likewise, Peter exclaims:

Praise be to the God and Father of our Lord Jesus
Christ! In his great mercy he has given us new birth
into *a living hope* through the resurrection of Jesus
Christ from the dead, and into an inheritance that
can never perish, spoil or fade. This inheritance
is kept in heaven for you, who through faith are

shielded by God's power until the coming of the salvation that is ready to be revealed in the last time.

In all this you greatly rejoice, though now for a little while you may have had to suffer grief in all kinds of trials. These have come so that the proven genuineness of your faith—of greater worth than gold, which perishes even though refined by fire—may result in praise, glory and honor when Jesus Christ is revealed.

This is it. This is our hope. This is what we hold on to. Peter continues:

Though you have not seen him, you love him; and even though you do not see him now, you believe in him and are filled with an inexpressible and glorious joy, for you are receiving the end result of your faith, the salvation of your souls. (1 Pet. 1:3–9 NIV 2011)

We haven't seen Him yet—you and I. Not face-to-face . But we will. It's what we live for. It's what we long for.

Until then, we're what the prophet Zechariah called "prisoners of hope."

Hope begins in the dark, the stubborn hope that if you just show up and try to do the right thing, the dawn will come. You wait and watch and work: You don't give up.

—Anne Lamott

After seventy years in exile, God's people rejoiced that they were finally free to return to their homeland. But Zechariah challenged them to keep their focus on the far greater hope, far greater joy, far greater deliverance, far greater freedom they would experience when their Messiah appeared:

> Rejoice greatly, O daughter of Zion!
>> Shout aloud, O daughter of Jerusalem!
> Behold, your king is coming to you;
>> righteous and having salvation is he,
> humble and mounted on a donkey. (Zech. 9:9 ESV)

Speaking prophetically on behalf of God, he said:

> Return to your stronghold, O prisoners of hope;
>> today I declare that I will restore to you double.
>> (Zech. 9:12 ESV)

God was their Fortress, their Stronghold, and they would find strength in Him as they held on to hope and waited . . . waited for the day He would come to them in power and glory!

We know that Jesus—the Messiah—has come, just as Zechariah prophesied. And the world rejoiced—greatly! But things are not yet what they will be. We who are alive today are waiting . . . waiting for His Second Coming, waiting for Him to return in power and glory.

In the meantime, we know His Spirit lives within us. We continue in the faith as we were taught, established and firm, not moving from "the hope held out in the gospel" (Col. 1:22–24). And, like the psalmist, we declare by faith: "The LORD will fulfill his purpose for me" (Ps. 138:8 ESV). While we wait, we find our strength in Him. He is our Rock, our Fortress, our Refuge, our Stronghold, our Shield, and our Deliverer.

> It is God who arms me with strength
>> and makes my way perfect.
> He makes my feet like the feet of a deer;
>> he enables me to stand on the heights.
> He trains my hands for battle;
>> my arms can bend a bow of bronze.
>> (Ps. 18:32–34)

He has promised us victory!

Our hope is not in ourselves, not in our strength, our wisdom, our talent, our ability. Not in our goodness, our righteousness, our purity. Not in our spiritual maturity. Our hope is not in our family, not in our friends. Our career, our achievements, or our successes. Our hope is not in our health or wealth, our power or prestige or influence. It's not in our education or ambition or visions or dreams. Our hope is not in science or the medical community. Our hope is not in our country or our national security.

Our hope is in Jesus—"the Son of God, who loved me and gave himself for me" (Gal. 2:20).

You know what? It turns out that holding on to hope is easy, after all. Because it's holding on to Jesus. And He says He's already holding on to you and me (Phil. 3:12).

> I give them eternal life, and they shall never perish;
> no one can snatch them out of my hand. (John 10:28)

Bible Study

1. When you think about heaven, when you think about eternity—what are the things you most look forward to? List your top ten. (If you have trouble coming up with ten, maybe you need a little refresher on what the Bible says we have to look forward to. Both Randy Alcorn and Joni Eareckson Tada have written fabulous books entitled *Heaven*.)

2. Read Romans 5:1–5. What do we rejoice in? Why? What (or who) is that hope rooted in? (Why doesn't it let us down or disappoint us or put us to shame?)

3. Look up 1 Peter 3:15–16. We live in a dark and dying world, full of lost souls. If one of them—a neighbor, a coworker, a friend—asked you the reason for the hope you have, what would you say? Take some time right now to articulate a thoughtful

answer—something simple, straightforward, and from the heart. Keep it personal to you and your experience (rather than a theological lecture).

4. Choose one of the following verses—or one mentioned previously in the chapter—to memorize and meditate on this week:

Psalm 42:11	Psalm 147:11
Romans 15:13	2 Thessalonians 2:16–17
Psalm 130:5	Romans 5:3–5
Hebrews 10:23	1 Peter 1:13

5. Take a few moments to record any further thoughts or reflections in your journal.

Afterword

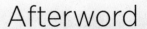

. . . the cure really is in the process, because you can't microwave spiritual growth.

—Jennifer Dukes Lee

You know the moment you give your heart to Jesus—the moment you put your faith in Him—you receive His salvation. But sanctification, the process of becoming more and more like Him, isn't so instantaneous.

Years ago, I ran across this profound observation by Bono, lead singer of the Irish rock band U2:

> Your nature is a hard thing to change; it takes time. One of the extraordinary transferences that happen in your spiritual life is not that your character flaws go away but they start to work for you. A negative becomes a positive: you've a big mouth—you end up a singer. You're insecure—you end up a performer who needs applause. I have heard of people having life-changing, miraculous turnarounds, people set free from addiction after a single prayer, relationships saved where both parties "let go, and let God." But it was not like that for me. For all that "I was lost, I am found," it is probably more accurate to say, "I was really lost, I'm a little less so at the moment." And then a little less and a little less again. That

> to me is the spiritual life. The slow reworking and
> rebooting of a computer at regular intervals, reading
> the small print of the service manual. It has slowly
> rebuilt me in a better image. It has taken years
> though, and it is not over yet.[1]

Not yet.

That's the biggest challenge, isn't it? Living between the now and the not yet. Trusting the process. Or, rather, trusting the One who guides the process. The One who leads us on this journey. And it is a journey—full of steps and stages, stops and starts. Sometimes it feels like it's two steps forward, one step back. Other days it feels like one step forward, two steps back!

We've talked a lot about the things we need to let go of. I think our vision of what our journey would or could or should look like is another one of those things. Our expectations for our own spiritual growth and the process God will use to produce it. Our schedule, our timetable. Our ideas and suggestions. Here instead are three thoughts I want to leave you with—three more things I want to encourage you to hold on to.

No matter what it looks like, no matter how it feels, you *are* making progress. You are! I promise you. Every day that you live and breathe. Every day that you get out of bed in the morning and put one foot in front of the other—and even on the days you don't. Even on those days you stay in bed and pull the covers over your head.

You're learning something. You're experiencing something that God can and will use for His glory and your good. Don't let yourself get discouraged by what seems to you to be a lack of progress. You don't see what God sees. You don't know what He knows.

Only He knows who you truly are in the very depths of your heart, mind, and soul. Only He understands just how far you've truly come. Only He can count every victory—every time you resisted temptation, or tried to. Every time you trusted Him when you didn't understand. Every time you made a good choice, or at least a better one. Every loving or patient or forgiving thought, every sacrificial act. Only He knows what it cost you and what you were willing to give.

Only God knows what He's trying to teach you . . . what this latest "test of your faith" really is (James 1:3).

You may think—for instance—that progress is not losing your temper at all today. God might say that progress is losing your temper less—or less easily—or biting your tongue when you've lost it. Progress could also mean being quicker to apologize after the fact. Or not giving up, after you've fallen or failed.

Then again, there could be progress in losing your temper so many times in a single day—despite your best effort, despite your most fervent resolve—that you finally realize you are utterly incapable of exercising even the tiniest amount of self-control and that you are desperate for and totally dependent on Him to help you. That realization could be the victory He's looking for. That humility. That whole new understanding and compassion for others who, like you, are powerless to change themselves. That tearful moment when your heart wells up with deepest gratitude that Jesus was willing to suffer and die to save a "wretch" like you. Like me.

See what I mean?

I once heard Dr. Tony Evans preach a powerful message in which he pointed out that the more sinful we feel—the more aware of our weaknesses, our faults and failings—the closer we may actually be to God! The closer we may be to spiritual maturity. He compared it to being in a dimly lit room, which looks pretty good at first glance. But you walk over to a lamp, and all of a sudden you can see all the dust, all the smudges, all the dirt and grime. They've been there the whole time. But the closer you are to the light, the more you see! And that's a very good thing. Being closer to the light, seeing things more clearly—it's a sign of progress all by itself.

It's only when you see it that you can deal with it, that you can take the next step in the process. And keep making progress.

There is a purpose for the process. There is a purpose *in* **the process.** It's not empty or meaningless. It's not futile. It's not a waste of time. Nothing in God's economy is wasted. Remember, He uses it all! The Scriptures are full of examples of how God patiently works in us and through us. How He teaches us and trains us. How He prepares us for the battles He knows we will face. How He tries and tests us. How He strengthens us and blesses us.

Look at David. Before the shepherd boy could become Israel's greatest king, he needed time. He needed experience. He needed to get some battles under his belt. He learned to depend on the power of God to enable him to fight a lion and a bear, long before he took on a giant. He learned to face down the criticism and accusation and condemnation of his brothers, before he could confidently stand up in front of his countrymen and lead them as their king.

It's true for you, too. Because of what you've been through in the past, because of what you're going through right now, you will be able to face whatever lies ahead. You will have the courage and confidence and conviction that God is with you. He was with you before. He will be with you again.

You will have learned to see His loving hand in everything that comes your way. To listen to His voice and follow His lead. You will be able to say with Job: "He knows the way that I take; when he has tested me, I will come forth as gold" (Job 23:10).

One day, you *will* reach the journey's end, and you will be the woman you were meant to be. One day you will be free. No matter how long it takes. No matter what it takes. It will happen. In Philippians 1:6, the Apostle Paul says: "I am convinced *and* sure of this very thing, that He Who began a good work in you will continue until the day of Jesus Christ [right up to the time of His return], developing [that good work] *and* perfecting *and* bringing it to full completion in you" (AMP).

He is faithful and He will not forget. He will never forsake His own.

One day you will stand in the presence of God. You'll see your True Love face to face. And all the guilt, shame, and regret, those impossible standards and unrealistic expectations, all the hurt, bitterness, and unforgiveness, the constant battle for control, the worry, the negativity, the misery, and all those lesser things that competed with Him for your love and devotion . . . once and for all, you will finally, completely, irrevocably let it go.

Forever and ever you will hold on to His amazing grace, unending freedom, total healing, perfect peace, overflowing joy, eternal hope, and everlasting love.

It will be so worth it—every trial or test you faced, every battle you fought, every tear you cried.

And it won't be long before that day comes. It'll be here before you know it. So until then, in light of this glorious truth. . . . "Since we are surrounded by so great a cloud of witnesses [who have borne testimony to the Truth], let us strip off *and* throw aside every encumbrance (unnecessary weight) and that sin which so readily (deftly and cleverly) clings to *and* entangles us, and let us run with patient endurance *and* steady *and* active persistence the appointed course of the race that is set before us, looking away [from all that will distract] to Jesus" (Heb. 12:1–2 AMP).

"Fixing our eyes on Jesus . . . " (Heb. 12:2).

Looking to Him. Focusing intently on Him.

Moment by moment. Hour by hour. Day by day.

When you do that, it's incredible how simple it is to take it all—everything else—and just let it go.

Leave it at His feet.

Questions Women Ask

How Do I Know If It's My Personality, Perfectionism, or OCD?

In Chapters Three and Four, we talked about letting go of impossible standards and unrealistic expectations. If this is an area in which just "letting it go" is particularly difficult for you, it could be a completely natural (if sometimes challenging) function of your personality—your God-given temperament. It could also be that you're battling perfectionism or obsessive-compulsive disorder (OCD). Understanding the difference can help you figure out the best strategy for learning to let it go.

Personality

Some of us seem to be born conscientious—deep thinkers who thrive on order and structure and logic. We focus intently on the pursuit of excellence and perfection. It's how God made us. As the saying goes, it's both a blessing and a curse. A strength and a weakness.

This personality type is one of four major types that have been identified and studied by experts for hundreds of years. Different people have come up with different names for it. It's alternately known as: the Melancholy, the Perfect Melancholy, the Conscientious, the Rational, the Thinking, or even the Beaver.

You may have had a chance to take a proper personality test (Facebook quizzes don't count!) at school or at work, at a professional conference, or at a church Bible study—the latter usually in conjunction with a curriculum designed to help you identify your spiritual gifts. If you haven't yet, you should think about it! You may find it simply confirms what you already know.

But it could also be life-changing. It might really help you to recognize, understand, accept, and appreciate the different aspects of your God-given personality. It could also help you understand why other people think and act the way they do.

The most reputable, well-known secular versions of the test go by names like the DiSC Profile, the Keirsey Temperament Sorter, and the Myers-Briggs Type Indicator. (The MBTI actually identifies sixteen distinct personality types, so try this one if none of the "big four" feels like a good fit for you.) Hugely popular Christian versions include the Personality Test by Gary Smalley and John Trent and Personality Plus by Florence Littauer.

Perfectionism

Experts tell us that regardless of whether we have that conscientious personality, we can all be perfectionists at certain times or about specific things. Perfectionism is defined as a personal standard, attitude, or philosophy of life that demands perfection—the highest excellence—and rejects anything less.

Psychologists say perfectionism can be an asset, to some extent, when it's self-oriented—when it motivates us to achieve and excel. (Think of the kind of focus and discipline and pursuit of excellence required by Olympic athletes, for instance.) But this kind of perfectionism can just as easily be damaging, when our standards are unreasonable or unachievable or become overwhelming to us.

Others-oriented perfectionism is *always* destructive, because others cannot and should not live their lives to please us; nor should they constantly be evaluated and subsequently criticized by us for failing to meet standards we set for them.

Just as devastating is socially-prescribed perfectionism—what we experience when we believe that other people have set these incredibly high standards and expectations for us—and that we *must* meet them. It's extreme people-pleasing.

Again, we've talked about some of these issues earlier in the book. I mention them here to point out that sometimes our perfectionism goes deep enough—and is damaging or destructive enough—that it triggers clinical depression (see the section "What about Antidepressants?") and that we may need professional help (see the next section, "When Do I Need an Accountability Partner, a Life Coach, or a Licensed Therapist?").

In this case, the smartest, wisest, bravest, strongest, most excellent and perfect thing we could possibly do is to humble ourselves, admit we need help, and ask for it. If your perfectionism is really taking a toll on you—if it's seriously impacting your life and the lives of those around you, talk to a trusted friend, a Christian counselor, a psychologist, or a psychiatrist.

It's especially important to seek help if your perfectionism has become full-blown OCD.

A Perfectionist with Obsessive-Compulsive Disorder (OCD)

An OCD perfectionist is obsessed with the need to accomplish specific tasks perfectly—and terrified of the thought of what will happen if she does not. In fact, fear is the dominant and driving emotion. Fear of failure, fear of disappointing others or letting them down or losing their good opinion of her.

For example, she will check and recheck her work, endlessly revising and redoing certain projects—convinced that she's missed something or made a mistake or that previous efforts simply weren't good enough. In some cases, her research and preparations will be so overly thorough that she never actually begins the task at hand.

She'll relive conversations, replay messages, or read emails over and over again, anxious that others have misunderstood or misconstrued her words. Eventually, she'll become exhausted and worn out, crippled, or paralyzed by the thought of taking on a project or reading a book or answering an email—or whatever triggers her obsessive behavior. So she just won't do it at all.

There's much more—a strong correlation between perfectionism and OCD and eating disorders, for instance—but if this could describe you or someone you love, please get help.

There are people who can help us see things we have difficulty seeing on our own—lies we've believed, faulty messages we've received. Unhealthy thoughts or ideas, attitudes, or behavior patterns.

Yes, Jesus can help us. He can heal us. I believe that all true healing and recovery starts and ends with Him. But I also believe that often He chooses to work through people He has gifted with special knowledge and skills and training. People He has called to walk alongside us, teach us, encourage us, and strengthen us.

We don't have to make this journey on our own.

When Do I Need an Accountability Partner, a Life Coach, or a Licensed Therapist?

Sometimes you need a little more help to let it go, to get unstuck, to learn to walk in freedom. As you've been reading this book, you may have come to the realization that you have some deeper issues to address. You may feel you need to get some additional support, encouragement, and advice—specific to you and your personal situation.

That's a great idea!

The Scriptures teach us that it's wise to seek godly counsel; they tell us that God has gifted members of the body of Christ to exhort, encourage, counsel, and advise one another. Some use their gifts on an informal basis; others get specialized training, certification, licensing, or advanced degrees, and they choose to make helping others their life's calling—their career and profession.

Depending on your needs, you might want to consider getting help from an accountability partner, a life coach, or a licensed therapist—a counselor or psychologist or psychiatrist.

Accountability Partner

An *accountability partner* is a trusted friend who agrees (at your request) to hold you accountable—to ask you to give an account of your attitudes, actions, or behaviors. It's to keep you honest, keep you on track, keep you moving forward. You voluntarily confess your sins and struggles to one another, share where you're experiencing growth and progress, and support each other with prayer and Scriptural encouragement.

Sometimes it's a fairly organized, structured arrangement. You agree to get together on a regular basis for an hour or two, each month or each week. You draw up a list of specific questions you want the other person to ask you, every time you meet. Or you show each other your journals or work through a book or Bible study together and spend some time in prayer. You might have one particular issue that is always the focus of your time together—the reason for your partnership—or it might be a more comprehensive, how-I'm-doing-in-my-life-overall kind of thing.

Your accountability can also be a much more fluid, sporadic, or spontaneous arrangement. For instance, you realize you've been procrastinating on a project or skipping your devotional time or exercise this week. So you text your friend and tell her what you plan to do to get back on track—and ask her to message you at the end of the week to see if you followed through. Or maybe you have a standing invitation to call your friend whenever you're really tempted to give in to that familiar sin. She promises to drop everything and pray with you until it passes and you've found your resolve again. Usually, if not always, this kind of accountability is a two-way street. A reciprocal, mutually beneficial arrangement.

When you're looking for an accountability partner, it's important to choose someone you know and trust. Someone who will keep your conversations confidential. Someone who will not judge or criticize or condemn you—but also someone who will not make excuses for you or let you off the hook. Sometimes having someone who battles the same things you do can work beautifully. Because you both get it. You understand what the other person is going through—and you can find solutions together. Other times it can work against you, if you just end up commiserating together, giving in and giving up together.

You may have an ideal accountability partner already living with you in your own home—in your own family. And if you do, that's wonderful! But honestly, family members don't always make the best accountability partners. Sometimes they're the biggest obstacles or the biggest contributors to your personal challenges. Even if they mean well and sincerely want to help you, it's too easy for them to slip into the role of parent or nanny. You start to feel like a naughty child who's constantly being scrutinized, criticized, or reprimanded. For the sake of your family relationships, it might be better to choose a friend instead—some would say two friends—to keep things objective and balanced and healthy.

Even so, over time you may discover that you're reluctant to be open and honest with your accountability partner. She might not be the right fit for you or she may not really have time for you. You may realize you need more help or a different kind of help than she can give. Or you may find yourself in a time and a place in your life where you don't have anyone you could ask to be your accountability partner. You might consider working with a life coach.

Life Coach

What is a *life coach*? A life coach is, well, a coach! A mentor, a cheerleader, and an accountability partner all in one. Life coaches are wellness support people in the same category as personal fitness trainers, nutritionists, or massage therapists.

Life coaches come alongside you to help you figure out where you are in your life, where you want to be, and what it will take to get there. They teach you how to identify your own strengths and weaknesses—what you need to reach your full potential. They brainstorm with you to define your goals and then break them down into practical, concrete steps you can take. And then they stay on you, to make sure you get those things done!

Life coaches typically meet with you on a regular basis either in person, over the phone, or through online video-conferencing (like Skype). You may sign up to work with a life coach for a certain number of sessions or for a specific length of time or until you accomplish a particular goal.

A life coach is different than counseling and therapy in a number of ways. For one thing, there's much more collaboration and camaraderie with a life coach. It's not as formal as a typical doctor-patient relationship. Life coaches like to say they stay focused on the present and the future—whereas therapists help you work through pain from the past. Therapists say that while they can do wellness and coaching, too, most of their work is with people who have addictions, personality disorders, post-traumatic stress, or other serious mental health issues. In short, therapists help patients move from a place of dysfunction to function; life coaches help people who function—more or less—at an ordinary level to learn how to function at their best.

Life coaching can be much more expensive than traditional therapy or counseling services. And it's not covered by insurance. The profession is also much less regulated. Just about anyone can call herself a life coach, so you want to be careful.

You may know someone who is naturally a fabulous mentor and motivator, someone who has decided to take that talent and turn it into a business by becoming a life coach. If you know that person well and feel comfortable with his or her level of expertise, that's probably fine. (And likely to be cheaper!) You're paying for help to organize your life—your calendar, your goals, your to-do list—the same way you might pay someone to help you organize your home office or your closets.

But unless you have that personal connection, you're going to want to look for a coach who has received a significant amount of specialized "coaching training," someone who has submitted themselves to the rigorous requirements of an organization like the International Coach Federation (ICF), in order to earn some type of official licensing or certification. Quite a few life coaches are actually former therapists, licensed counselors, or psychologists, so you know that they have had extensive education and experience. Many of them are Christians who have a passion for mentoring, encouraging others in their spiritual growth and development.

If you're not able to move forward with the help of a life coach—if it becomes clear that you've got some emotional trauma or more serious mental health issues you're dealing with—a responsible life coach will not attempt to counsel you or treat you for those issues. It's not their area of expertise! Instead, they will refer you to a professional therapist—a licensed counselor or psychologist or psychiatrist.

Licensed Therapist

The difference between licensed mental healthcare profession-als is not so much the types of patients or conditions they treat as it is their educational background and training. For example, a *licensed counselor* or *clinical social worker* holds a master's degree and has completed a minimum two-year internship. A *psychologist* has earned a doctorate—a PhD—followed by a two-year internship. A *psychiatrist* has graduated from medical school first and then taken an additional four years of advanced training, specializing in mental health.

Only psychiatrists (because they are medical doctors) include physical exams and medical tests in their evaluations. They're the ones who could determine whether or not your psychological symptoms have actually resulted from a brain injury or some other type of physical illness or disease. Only psychiatrists can prescribe medication—and that usually ends up being their focus. They frequently work in clinics and hospital settings. But even in private practice, while they do some counseling, it's mostly about managing medications for patients who need these kinds of interventions.

Which type of licensed professional you see really depends on what your needs are and who's available to you in your area. For instance, all of these professionals are qualified to help you address your anxiety or depression or anger issues. But they may specialize in one issue or another. Some have more experience with marriage and family counseling, while others have more experience treating eating disorders. If you require medication, you'll need a medical doctor to prescribe it for you. You can either get it from your family physician working in conjunction with your psychologist, or you can get it directly from your psychiatrist.

The specific type of doctor or degree isn't as important as their overall experience and training. You just want to find someone who's qualified and competent. Someone you feel comfortable confiding in. Someone you feel confident can help you. Ideally, you hope to find a Christian counselor whose advice and encouragement will be thoroughly grounded in Scripture. But if not, at least a counselor who is familiar with and respectful of your faith.

So how do you find a good counselor or therapist? Start by praying! Ask God to lead you every step of the way. Then ask people you trust—your friends, your family, your doctor, your pastor—for their recommendations. Get as many as you can. And do your homework. Look up the websites of potential counselors or therapists. Check out their qualifications, their years of experience, and their areas of expertise.

You can also find referrals through the American Association of Christian Counselors (www.aacc.net/resources/find-a-counselor) and the National Christian Counselors Association (www.ncca.org/Directory/search.aspx). Focus on the Family has a free counseling hotline. They can also connect you with a reputable Christian counselor in your area. (Call 1-855-771-HELP or visit www.focusonthefamily.com/counseling/find-a-counselor.aspx.)

Some churches have professional counselors on staff or counseling ministries involving "lay counselors"—members of the congregation who are mature believers and have been through a comprehensive biblical counseling program. Most pastors do offer counseling as well, and pastoral counseling is usually free. One thing to keep in mind: there are many wonderful, godly pastors who have a lot of wisdom, a lot of experience in ministry. They have a heart for hurting people, a heart for counseling, as well as a real gift for it—to which many of them add special training to enable them to be even more effective at helping others. But some pastors, well . . . don't.

So, whenever possible, it's best to get a personal recommendation from someone you trust. And if the first counselor you see isn't as helpful as you hoped, don't give up. Try again. Your healing—your freedom—is worth fighting for!

What about Antidepressants?

All of us experience moments of disappointment, discouragement, and defeat. Feelings of hopelessness and helplessness. Especially following a time of crisis or trauma, when we've been undergoing major life changes or coping with grief and loss. Sometimes these moments can last for days, weeks, or even months.

If you've been exhibiting the following symptoms on a daily basis—for some time—you might be suffering from depression:

- Feelings of sadness, emptiness, or unhappiness.
- Angry outbursts, irritability, or frustration, even over small matters.
- Loss of interest or pleasure in normal activities.
- Sleep disturbances, including insomnia or sleep-ing too much.

- Tiredness and lack of energy, so that even small tasks take extra effort.
- Changes in appetite—often reduced appetite and weight loss, but increased cravings for food and weight gain in some people.
- Anxiety, agitation, or restlessness—for example, excessive worrying, pacing, hand-wringing, or inability to sit still.
- Slowed thinking, speaking, or body movements.
- Feelings of worthlessness or guilt, fixating on past failures, or blaming yourself for things that are not your responsibility.
- Trouble thinking, concentrating, making decisions, and remembering things.
- Frequent thoughts of death, suicidal thoughts, or suicide attempts.
- Unexplained physical problems, such as back pain or headaches.[1]

Some Christians have serious reservations about taking medication to treat depression. If the problem is in essence spiritual, then shouldn't it be addressed from a spiritual perspective and on a spiritual basis? Others feel that since there may be physical causes or at least physical symptoms that coincide with the spiritual issues, medication can be an effective—even lifesaving—tool.

Since the Scripture doesn't say "thou shalt" or "thou shalt not," I think each one of us is responsible to consider prayerfully how we believe God is leading us.

What Healthcare Professionals Tell Us

Antidepressants can provide some relief to people suffering from severe depression. Notice the words "can" and "some." These drugs are not a miracle cure; they do not work for everyone. In fact, recent studies suggest that fewer than 50 percent of people who take antidepressants become symptom-free, and many of them soon experience the return of their symptoms while they are still taking the medication. For some people, antidepressants actually have the opposite effect; they increase the risk of suicide or suicidal thoughts.

Most doctors prescribe antidepressants for a minimum of six months to a year, because it can take that long to find the right drug or combination of drugs, experience the benefits, and adjust to the side effects. In addition, many antidepressants are addictive, in the sense that the body becomes accustomed to them and experiences withdrawal symptoms if they are stopped abruptly—which is why doctors advise a gradual tapering off of the medication. With all of the potential complications, side effects, and drug interactions, most doctors do not recommend the indefinite use of antidepressants unless there is another underlying mental health issue, such as bipolar disorder.

Antidepressant medications are most effective when taken under close medical supervision and in conjunction with life-style changes (such as improved nutrition, exercise, counseling, or therapy). At their best, they work like training wheels on a bicycle. They give you a little stability—for a time—so you can climb up in the saddle and start pedaling again. The goal is to get you back to riding on your own.

So are antidepressants right for you?

Is your depression severe? In other words, is it significantly interfering with your ability to function on a daily basis? (For instance, you might be finding excuses not to leave the house. Or you might find yourself tempted to self-medicate with drugs or alcohol. You may be battling insomnia or wrestling with suicidal thoughts. You may even experience hallucinations.) For mild depression, lifestyle changes may be enough.

Are you prepared to risk the potential side effects of medication? Do you have a plan in place to get the spiritual help and support you need as well? Have you prayed about your decision? Talked to your family? Your doctor?

If you do decide to move forward, make sure your doctor also has a clear plan in mind—which medication he or she will prescribe and for how long. Keep a journal in which you carefully track your medication, dosage, side effects, and symptoms.

And keep looking to Jesus. Ultimately all of our help, our hope, and our healing comes from Him.

How Can I Help a Child or Grandchild Battling Perfectionism?

Some children are born perfectionists and others are made. It's more likely if they're firstborn, or if they're sensitive or gifted, or if they (ahem!) have a perfectionist parent modeling the behavior for them.

Here's a glimpse of what perfectionism looks like in children:

- Constantly comparing themselves—their appearance, their performance, their accomplishments and achievements—to others.

- Judging themselves (and sometimes others) harshly; criticizing or condemning themselves for perceived failures.
- Worrying that whatever work they've done, it won't be good enough. Redoing their assignments over and over and over again, trying (and failing, by their estimation) to get things "just right."
- Procrastinating or avoiding projects altogether, out of fear of failure, or in dread of the enormous effort they know it will take to complete it to their own exacting standards.
- Focusing on their failures instead of their successes; counting how many things they got wrong, not how many they got right.
- Insisting that there is only one "right" way to do something and becoming extremely agitated when challenged to accept other approaches.
- Finding it hard to laugh at themselves or their mistakes.
- Avoiding trying new things, because they're afraid they might not be good at them.

When all of this fear and worry and frustration and stress builds up, it frequently leads to emotional outbursts—meltdowns or temper tantrums. But it can also manifest itself physically. Children battling perfectionism often suffer from headaches, stomachaches, teeth-grinding, and trouble sleeping at night.

It's one thing to battle perfectionism ourselves; it's another to watch a child wrestle with it. Our hearts go out to them. We know how hard it is. We may feel helpless. So many parents and grandparents have looked for ways to help their children. A quick Internet search will pull up dozens of articles and websites full of ideas and practical suggestions.

A Few Basics

Pray. And then pray. And then pray some more. Seriously! Ask God for wisdom every single day, with every single incident or issue that comes up. Every child is different, every situation is different. It takes so much wisdom to know what to do and what not to do, what to say and what not to say. To find the balance between encouraging children to do their best and reach their full potential—and teaching them to understand that it's okay to fall and fail, because that's how we learn, that's how we grow. Thankfully, God promises to give us all the wisdom we need, if we ask for it! (James 1:5).

Learn to challenge your own perfectionism and lead by example. Teach your child the same principles, the same Scriptures, the same strategies that are helping you. Just adapt them a little—use examples and illustrations that are age-appropriate. (See Chapters Three and Four.) Live out loud the life skills—the thoughts, the attitudes, the behaviors—you want them to learn. And keep in mind the following dos and don'ts.

DO encourage children to discover and develop their own unique, God-given talents. Give them opportunities to explore a wide variety of interests and activities, to help them find areas they are gifted in, along with the understanding that *no one* is gifted at everything. And you can still enjoy something, even if you're not gifted at it. But you don't know what you can do until you try!

DON'T overschedule children with too many extracurricular activities all at once; don't let your fears for their future or regrets about your past cause you to push them to do too much or try too hard. Don't create unrealistic expectations for them. Don't set them up to fail.

DO focus on the positive. Emphasize growth and progress and improvement—which is always the goal—rather than the end result. Remember, we're talking about children who make themselves physically ill when they can't "win" or get it "just right." Praise character (courage, kindness, generosity) or effort (persistence, determination) rather than outcome. And encourage them to praise those things in others.

DON'T publicly compare your children's achievements or performance to others, and don't encourage them to compare themselves. It's about doing or being your best, not about being better (or worse) than someone else.

DO listen compassionately to children's fears and frustrations. Encourage them to open up and be honest with you about what they're thinking and feeling.

DON'T dismiss their feelings—but don't be afraid to challenge negative thinking. For instance, you might say, "You're not a failure. You're not a loser. The world is not coming to an end because you missed a problem on the test. Everybody makes mistakes. Yes, you can learn how to do this—and I'll help you!"

DO identify a few key Scriptures or kid-friendly motivational sayings that you can make your family mottos. For instance, "I can do all things through Christ!" (Phil. 4:13 KJV)

or "Whether you think you can or you can't, you're right!" or
"Keep moving forward!" Post them around the house and say
them to each other on a daily basis.

Find ways to continually fill your home and your hearts
with God's Truth, to counteract the enemy's lies. Here are
some more ideas . . .

Music for Young Children

I used to be a preschool and elementary school teacher, and
when I was teaching in Christian schools, I loved to keep praise
and worship music playing softly in the background throughout
the day. It made my classroom feel like a warm, happy, safe
place to be. It had such a positive influence on my students!
I'd often hear the children singing the words of the songs in
the hallway or on the playground—even though we'd never
made a conscious effort to learn them. I often caught myself
singing them, too!

Playtime, naptime, drive-time, nighttime—these are all
good times to strengthen our hearts and nourish our spirits
with the truth of God's Word. These are a few of my personal
favorites for young children. (All of these albums are available
on iTunes and online sources.)

> *Kids of the Kingdom* and *Follow the Leader*
> —Annie Herring
> *The Donut Man—Songs That Teach, Songs That*
> *Praise* series—Rob Evans
> *The Praise Baby Collection*—Brentwood Music
> *Hide 'Em in Your Heart: Bible Memory Melodies,*
> *Vols. 1 and 2*—Steve Green

Sleep Sound In Jesus: Gentle Lullabies for Baby
    —Michael Card
Bedtime Prayers: Lullabies and Peaceful Worship
    —Twila Paris

If you have older children, encourage them to create their own playlists—songs that remind them to be joyful, to be patient, to be persistent, to have courage and confidence in the Lord!

Books, Movies, and More

Keep your eyes open for age-appropriate books and movies about real-life people who faced failure, discouragement, and defeat—but didn't give up—and eventually experienced victory. There are lots of these stories from the world of sports and science, art and music and history. The children's section of your local library will usually have a wide selection of biographies—picture books for little kids and longer books for middle grade readers—that you can check out together. (I've written a few myself!)

I also love the Disney animated movie *Meet the Robinsons* and Pixar's *The Incredibles* and *Monsters University*—because the message of these films is so different from the one most children's movies preach. These movies acknowledge that no matter how much you believe in yourself, you will not be able to do everything you want to do—or do everything you want to do perfectly. But you can still accomplish some pretty amazing things, if you find what God has uniquely gifted you to do—and if you don't give up, if you aren't afraid to fail.

Glynnis Whitwer has provided another fabulous resource for parents with her book *When Your Child Is Hurting: Helping*

Your Kids Survive the Ups and Downs of Life (Harvest House, 2009).

A Note on Perfectionism in Tweens and Teens

Recent studies have shown that young women who battle perfectionism seem much more likely to develop serious eating disorders such as anorexia and bulimia. They may also be more likely to engage in cutting and other kinds of self-harm. (Increasingly, young men are developing these behaviors, too.)

Unfortunately, there's not enough space here to go into all the reasons and risk factors and warning signs. Let me just share a few things.

The devastating spiritual, emotional, and psychological issues—and the destructive behaviors that accompany them—are far easier to prevent than they are to treat.

If you know you have a young perfectionist in your family, be aware of the special traps the enemy sets for them. Pray for them. Speak God's truth over them. Remind them daily who they are in Him—that they are already chosen, already loved, already cherished by Him. There's nothing they have to prove, nothing they need to achieve or accomplish in order to be worthy, in order to be "enough." They are already "enough" in Him.

You might consider getting together once a week or once a month for breakfast or lunch or a night out. Build your relationship by spending some special one-on-one time together—time in which you can have conversations about body image issues and peer pressure and perfectionism and whatever else they're going through. Read a book or do a Bible study together. (I recommend *Made to Crave for Young Women* by Lysa TerKeurst and Shaunti Feldhahn and *Love Idol* by Jennifer Dukes Lee—but there are countless others, many specifically for tweens or teens.) Keep your eyes open for teachable moments in everyday life.

If you think your young perfectionist may already have a serious issue—if they seem obsessively preoccupied with their appearance, weight, food intake, or exercise, if they seem continually anxious, moody, depressed, or withdrawn, and if they've been a victim of crime, abuse, or neglect or experienced major life trauma recently (death, divorce, a painful breakup), or if they frequently have unexplained injuries on their arms or legs—GET HELP.

No one simply outgrows eating disorders or self-harming behaviors. They do not go away on their own. Listen to that gut feeling, that voice that tells you all is not well. It may be the Holy Spirit.

Act on it.

If you look, you'll find there are tons of free resources available to you online—helpful articles and websites, organizations, and support groups. You can call the confidential hotline of the National Eating Disorder Association (NEDA) or visit their website, www.nationaleatingdisorders.org.

Ask your pastor or your family physician or school psychologist for a referral to a Christian counselor in your area who specializes in working with teens or eating disorders or both.

There is hope. There is healing.

Be willing to seek it out and fight for it, on behalf of those you love (Jer. 29:13; Neh. 4:14).

What Are Some Key Scriptures I Can Memorize?

There are countless Scriptures that encourage us to let go of the things that hold us back and hold on to the things that help us grow. Meditating on these Scriptures (really reflecting on their meaning and applying them to our lives) as well as memorizing them can help us finally be free to be the women we were created to be. Ideally, you want to choose the verses that speak most powerfully and personally to you.

A Few Verses to Get You Started

Forget the former things; do not dwell on the past. See, I am doing a new thing! Now it springs up; do you not perceive it? I am making a way in the wilderness and streams in the wasteland. (Isa. 43:18–19)

If we confess our sins, he is faithful and just and will forgive us our sins and purify us from all unrighteousness. (1 John 1:9)

So now there is no condemnation for those who belong to Christ Jesus. (Rom. 8:1 NLT)

Those who look to him are radiant; their faces are never covered with shame. (Ps. 34:5)

Let us then approach the throne of grace with confidence, so that we may receive mercy and find grace to help us in our time of need. (Heb. 4:16)

Being confident of this, that he who began a good work in you will carry it on to completion until the day of Christ Jesus. (Phil. 1:6)

He said to me, "My grace is sufficient for you, for my power is made perfect in weakness." Therefore I will boast all the more gladly about my weaknesses, so that Christ's power may rest on me. That is why, for Christ's sake, I delight in weaknesses, in insults, in hardships, in persecutions, in difficulties. For when I am weak, then I am strong. (2 Cor. 12:9–10)

But one thing I do: Forgetting what is behind and straining toward what is ahead, I press on toward the goal to win the prize for which God has called me heavenward in Christ Jesus. (Phil. 3:13–14)

Therefore we do not lose heart. Though outwardly we are wasting away, yet inwardly we are being renewed day by day. For our light and momentary troubles are achieving for us an eternal glory that far outweighs them all. So we fix our eyes not on what is seen, but on what is unseen, since what is seen is temporary, but what is unseen is eternal. (2 Cor. 4:16–18 NIV 2011)

"For I know the plans I have for you," declares the LORD, "plans to prosper you and not to harm you, plans to give you hope and a future." (Jer. 29:11)

Therefore, since we are surrounded by such a great cloud of witnesses, let us throw off everything that hinders and the sin that so easily entangles, and let us run with perseverance the race marked out for us. (Heb. 12:1)

He knows the way that I take; when he has tested
me, I will come forth as gold. (Job 23:10)

Recommended Resources

It can be the challenge of a lifetime, learning to let go of all the things that hold us back—and to hold on to the things that move us forward. The good news is that we're not alone. And there are a lot of great resources available to us. In addition to those I've mentioned in the text and the notes, I've included a few more in this section that—keeping our theme in mind—have been especially helpful to me.

For Reading

Books on believing, receiving, and experiencing God's grace

What's So Amazing About Grace?—Philip Yancey (Zondervan, 2002)

The Ragamuffin Gospel: Good News for the Bedraggled, Beat-Up, and Burnt Out—Brennan Manning (Multnomah, 2005)

Grace for the Good Girl: Letting Go of the Try-Hard Life—Emily P. Freeman (Revell, 2011)

Deceived by Shame, Desired by God—Cynthia Spell Humbert (NavPress, 2001)

Love Idol: Letting Go of Your Need for Approval and Seeing Yourself through God's Eyes—Jennifer Dukes Lee (Tyndale, 2014)

One Thousand Gifts Devotional: Reflections on Finding Everyday Graces—Ann Voskamp (Zondervan, 2012)

Books on relationships—letting go of bitterness and unforgiveness, experiencing healing, and setting healthy boundaries

No More Christian Nice Girl: When Being Nice—Instead of Good—Hurts You, Your Family, and Your Friends—Paul Coughlin and Jennifer D. Degler (Bethany House, 2010)

Wounded by God's People—Anne Graham Lotz (Zondervan, 2013)

Avoiding the 12 Relationship Mistakes Women Make—Georgia Shaffer (Harvest House, 2014)

The Emotionally Destructive Relationship: Seeing It, Stopping It, Surviving It—Leslie Vernick (Waterbrook, 2007)

The Emotionally Destructive Marriage: How to Find Your Voice and Reclaim Your Hope—Leslie Vernick (Waterbrook, 2013)

The Stronghold of God: Finding God's Place of Immunity from Attacks of the Enemy—Francis Frangipane (Charisma House, 1998)

Books on finding freedom (along with grace)

Lord, I Just Want to Be Happy—Leslie Vernick (Harvest House
  Publishers, 2009)

Idol Lies: Facing the Truth about Our Deepest Desires—Dee
  Brestin (Integrity, 2012)

*Made to Crave: Satisfying Your Deepest Desires with God, Not
  Food*—Lysa TerKeurst (Zondervan, 2010)

A Hunger for God: Desiring God through Fasting and Prayer—
  John Piper (Crossway, 1997)

Altar'd: Experience the Power of the Resurrection—Jennifer
  Kennedy Dean (New Hope, 2012)

*Unquenchable: Grow a Wildfire Faith That Will Endure
  Anything*—Carol Kent (Zondervan, 2014)

*Books that encourage focused spiritual growth without all
the stress and striving*

My One Word: Change Your Life with Just One Word—Mike
  Ashcraft and Rachel Olson (Zondervan, 2012)

Live These Words: An Active Response to God—Lucinda Secrest
  McDowell (Bold Vision, 2014)

For Watching

Les Miserables / *Les Mis* (1935, 1978, 1998, 2010, 2012)

Such a powerful story of grace and redemption! Watch any
of the movie versions, including the Andrew Lloyd Webber
musical. Or if you're very brave (or have a lot of time on your
hands) try reading the English translation of the original 1,200-
page novel by Victor Hugo.

Chariots of Fire (1981)
A true story about athletes who competed in the 1924 Olympic Games. Some were driven by a desire for fame and fortune, others by a desperate need to prove themselves, defy expectations (their own or others'), and triumph over those who doubted them. To achieve victory, they had to learn what to let go of and what to hold on to—and where to find the strength to finish the race.

Meet the Robinsons (2007)
A fabulously funny and heartwarming Disney movie about letting go of the past and celebrating your failures as well as your successes, so you can "keep moving forward!"

Groundhog Day (1993)
In light of my own elusive dream (see the Introduction), I couldn't resist adding this one—a movie about a guy who's doomed to live the same day over and over again, until he gets it right. He learns some surprisingly powerful and profound lessons along the way.

For Listening

The Bible
There are many different audio versions of Scripture available, in a variety of translations and formats (MP3, CD, DVD). You can choose the entire Bible, the Old Testament, the New Testament, just one particular book of the Bible, or even a selection of devotional Scripture readings. Try to listen to a few online or at your local Christian bookstore, to see whether you prefer

a "dramatized" version (with passages acted out by different actors and dramatic background music) or simple narration.

Music for Your Playlists

You may already have a number of much-loved songs or albums that you listen to when you need to be reminded what to let go of and what to hold on to, when your soul needs to hear some Truth. But if you're looking for some new songs to add to your playlist, keeping our theme in mind, here are a few of my personal favorites. (You could also use these songs as part of your "Letting It Go" Bible study, small group, or women's retreat.)

Album

So I Can Tell by Cheri Keaggy

Songs

"I Choose Grace"—Twila Paris

"Were It Not for Grace"—Larnelle Harris

"Amazing Grace"—Walela

"He Looked Beyond My Fault"—Sandi Patty

"Grace By Which I Stand"—Keith Green

"He Covers Me"—Steve Camp

"Be Still My Soul (In You I Rest)"—Kari Jobe

"Nobody Knows Me Like You"—Benny Hester

"In Christ Alone"—Keith & Kristyn Getty

"Lord of the Past"—Bob Bennett

"God Almighty"—Matthew Ward

"He's All You Need"—Steve Camp

"Child of the Father"—Cheri Keaggy

"Come and Fill My Heart"—Avalon

"I Want to Be More Like Jesus"—Keith Green

"Jesus, All for Jesus"—Sheila Walsh

"Oh Lord, You're Beautiful"—Keith Green

"Father, Hear Your Children"—Steve Green

"I Will Listen"—Twila Paris

"This Good Day"—Fernando Ortega

"My One Thing"—Rich Mullins

"A Different Road"—Kathy Troccoli

"You Never Let Go"—Matt Redman

Praise and worship, hymns, classical music, instrumental music, and even your favorite movie soundtracks can also be motivating, uplifting, and inspiring! There are a couple of upbeat secular songs I've added to my own playlist because they repeat some of the key words and phrases I want ringing in my heart:

"Little Wonders"—Rob Thomas

"Let It Go"—Idina Menzel

"Get Up"—Superchick

"A New Day Has Come"—Celine Dion

"Beautiful Day"—U2

Find what blesses your heart or ministers to your spirit most, and listen to it as often as you can.

Notes

Chapter One

1. *Pride and Prejudice*, directed by Simon Langton (A&E, 1995), DVD.

2. U2, "Stuck in a Moment That You Can't Get Out Of," by U2, Universal-Polygram International Publishing, Inc., 2001.

3. Horatio G. Spafford, "It Is Well with My Soul," public domain, 1873.

4. Brennan Manning, *The Ragamuffin Gospel: Good News for the Bedraggled, Beat-Up, and Burnt Out* (Sisters, OR: Multnomah, 2005), 117.

5. Ibid.

6. Philip Yancey, interview by Laura Bagby, "Philip Yancey: Hinting at God," CBN.com, www.cbn.com/spirituallife/biblestudyandtheology /perspectives/bagby-philip_yancey_0803.aspx.

7. See, for instance, Colossians 3:12, Zechariah 2:8, Ephesians 2:10, 1 Peter 2:9, Psalm 139, Ephesians 5:27, Romans 8:28–30, and 2 Corinthians 3:18.

Chapter Two

1. Spiros Zodhiates, ed., *Hebrew-Greek Key Word Study Bible, New International Version* (Chattanooga, TN: AMG International, 1996), 1619.

2. Ibid.

Chapter Three

1. Susie Steiner, "Top Five Regrets of the Dying," *The Guardian*, February 1, 2012, www.theguardian.com/lifeandstyle/2012/feb/01 /top-five-regrets-of-the-dying.

2. Christin Ditchfield, *What Women Should Know about Facing Fear* (Abilene, TX: Leafwood, 2013), 43–44.

3. Emily P. Freeman, *Grace for the Good Girl* (Grand Rapids, MI: Revell, 2011), 137.

4. Cathy Guisewite, *I Am Woman, Hear Me Snore: A Cathy Collection* (Kansas City, MO: Andrews-McMeel, 1998).

5. Oswald Chambers, "Taking the Initiative against Despair," in *My Utmost for His Highest, Updated Edition*, ed. James Reimann (Grand Rapids, MI: Discovery House, 1992), February 18.

Chapter Four

1. Robert Lopez and Kristen Anderson-Lopez, "Let It Go," performed by Idina Menzel, Walt Disney Records, 2013.

Chapter Five

1. Nancy Leigh DeMoss, *Choosing Forgiveness: Your Journey to Freedom* (Chicago: Moody, 2006), 215.

2. Corrie ten Boom, *I'm Still Learning to Forgive* (Wheaton, IL: Good News, 1995), quoted in Christin Ditchfield, *A Way with Words: What Women Should Know about the Power They Possess* (Wheaton, IL: Crossway, 2010), 33–34.

Chapter Six

1. Corrie ten Boom with Jamie Buckingham, *Tramp for the Lord* (Grand Rapids, MI: Revell, 1974), 272–76.

2. Anne Graham Lotz, *Wounded by God's People* (Grand Rapids, MI: Zondervan, 2013), 81.

3. On his website, Dr. Keith M. Kent shares three different versions of the "Paradoxical Commandments" that have been attributed to Mother Teresa—two that are said to be displayed on the walls of her orphanage in Calcutta and one that has appeared online (titled "The Final Analysis")— along with the original version Kent wrote for his leadership students in 1968. I chose the wording of each "commandment" that resonated most with me. For more information, see www.paradoxicalcommandments .com/mother-teresa-connection.html.

Chapter Eight

1. Brett James, Hillary Lindsey, and Gordie Sampson, "Jesus, Take the Wheel," performed by Carrie Underwood, SONY/ATV Music Publishing, Windswept Holdings, BMG Rights Management, US, 1995.

2. Lucinda Secrest McDowell, *Spa for the Soul: Rejuvenate Your Inner Life* (Nashville, TN: CrossBooks, 2009), 6.

3. I first heard Jennifer Kennedy Dean teach on this passage and principle of prayer at a conference several years ago. I wrote a blog post sharing what I recall from her message at http://www.christinditchfield .com/2013/06/he-knows-our-need/.

Chapter Nine

1. Bill Watterson, *The Complete Calvin and Hobbes: Book Two* (Kansas City, MO: Andrews McMeel, 2005), 376.

2. Dr. and Mrs. Howard Taylor, *James Hudson Taylor: A Biography* (London: Hodder & Stoughton, 1997).

3. Georgia Shaffer, *Avoiding the 12 Relationship Mistakes Women Make* (Eugene, OR: Harvest House, 2014), 89.

4. Carole Lewis, *A Thankful Heart: How an Attitude of Gratitude Brings Hope and Healing to Our Lives* (Ventura, CA: Regal Books, 2005), 21.

5. Ibid, 10.

Chapter Ten

1. L. B. Cowman, *Streams in the Desert*, Updated Edition, ed. James Reimann (Grand Rapids, MI: Zondervan, 1997), March 20.

2. Emily P. Freeman, *Grace for the Good Girl* (Grand Rapids, MI: Revell, 2011), 137.

Chapter Eleven

1. William P. Merrill, "Rise Up, O Men of God," public domain, 1911.

2. From the *Westminster Shorter Catechism*: Q. 1. What is the chief end of man? A. Man's chief end is to glorify God, [a] and to enjoy Him forever. [b] ~ [a]. Ps. 86:9; Isa. 60:21; Rom. 11:36; 1 Cor. 6:20; 10:31; Rev. 4:11 [b]. Ps. 16:5–11; 144:15; Isa. 12:2; Luke 2:10; Phil. 4:4; Rev. 21:3–4.

3. Henri J. M. Nouwen, *Bread for the Journey: A Daybook of Wisdom and Faith* (New York: HarperOne, 1994), April 23.

4. C.S. Lewis. *Christian Reflections.* (Grand Rapids: Wm. B. Eerdmans, 1967), 33.

5. Steve Camp, "Run to the Battle," performed by Steve Camp, Word Music, 1981.

6. *The Lord of the Rings: The Fellowship of the Ring*, directed by Peter Jackson (Los Angeles: New Line Cinema, 2001), DVD.

Chapter Twelve

1. *The Lord of the Rings: The Two Towers*, directed by Peter Jackson (Los Angeles: New Line Cinema, 2002), DVD.

Afterword

1. U2 with Neil McCormick, *U2 by U2* (New York: HarperCollins, 2006), 7.

What about Antidepressants?

1. "Depression: Symptoms," Mayo Clinic website, www.mayoclinic.org /diseases-conditions/depression/basics/symptoms/con-20032977.

CHRISTIN DITCHFIELD
Calling Women to a Deeper Life

A Note from Christin

Hi, I'm Christin Ditchfield. I'm a writer and a speaker. I host a syndicated daily radio program. I'm passionate about calling women to a deeper life—the kind of life that's found in a deeper relationship with Jesus Christ. It's the kind of life we long for, the kind of life we were created for.

Over the years, I've met so many women like me: women who love Jesus, but sometimes feel overwhelmed or distracted or disconnected from Him. Together we're learning how to walk with Him on a daily basis, so that we can experience a richer, deeper, more meaningful relationship with Him.

I've had the privilege of writing sixty-seven books (so far!), three of them with *What Women Should Know* in the title:

A Way with Words: What Women Should Know about the Power They Possess (Crossway, 2010)

What Women Should Know about Facing Fear (Leafwood, 2013)

What Women Should Know about Letting It Go (Leafwood, 2015)

These are the books of my heart—all the things I've been learning on my own spiritual journey over the last twenty-five years. It's my hope and prayer that they will be a blessing, an encouragement to you—wherever you are in yours.

These days, there are so many ways we can stay connected.

You can stop by my blog:

> http://ChristinDitchfield.com

Or listen to the radio broadcasts:

> http://TakeItToHeartRadio.com

Or follow me on:

http://facebook.com/christinditchfield

https://twitter.com/AuthorChristin

http://pinterest.com/authorchristin

I'm looking forward to hearing from you!

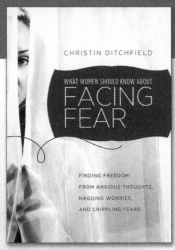